Big Joe:
The Joe Corrigan Story

Joe Corrigan
with
David Clayton

Fort Publishing Ltd

First published in 2008 by Fort Publishing Ltd, Old Belmont House,
12 Robsland Avenue, Ayr, KA7 2RW

Produced by Polskabook Ltd

Front-cover photograph courtesy of PA Photos

Graphic design by Mark Blackadder

Typeset by 3btype.com

ISBN: 978-1-905769-11-7

I would like to dedicate the book to my wife Val, daughters Sara and Emma and my son Andrew, not forgetting my wonderful grandchildren, Thomas, Victoria and Joseph, also known as the 'Little Rascals'.

Contents

Foreword

By
Bert Trautmann OBE

I am very proud to have been given the opportunity to introduce Joe Corrigan's autobiography for a number of reasons. My former colleague Frank Swift was a great goalkeeper, an England international and captain and I believe Joe Corrigan was equally as good as Frank.

I don't think any club in the country over the last forty years have had as good a set of goalkeepers as Manchester City had in Frank, Joe and, if you will permit me, Bert Trautmann.

I was the smallest of the trio, but the sheer presence of Frank and Joe must have struck fear into the oncoming strikers – they were giants! Joe was a great catcher of the ball, and, despite the fact that he was very tall he was excellent on the ground, too. I class him as one of the greatest goalkeepers of his day and when I try and compare him to modern-day goalkeepers, I find there is no-one who matches his quality.

We were all down-to-earth people, we loved the game and as a keeper you have to have a little bit of everything. You have to be a bit of a dare-devil, be able to make quick decisions and you have to recover from your mistakes.

I once saw Joe concede a goal from the halfway line and could see his confidence ebbing away as the game went on, so after the match I told him that I had seven goals put past me in my third game for City and once conceded eight! Another great goalkeeper, Harry Gregg, had nine put past him in his first game! It is something you must assess and then learn from.

We all have various trials and tribulations to overcome, but it is important to learn from your mistakes and come back stronger – a goalkeeper must have a big heart and Joe Corrigan most certainly had a big heart.

He was unfortunate to be up against two more fantastic English keepers in Peter Shilton and Ray Clemence during his career. Throughout the Seventies and early Eighties, England were blessed with three great goalkeepers, but of course, they couldn't all play and in that respect, Joe suffered on the international stage.

Without Shilton and Clemence around, he would have won 100 caps or more for his country, I believe. However, I've always felt that it is not how many international caps gained that great players should be measured against. I never represented my country, but it never altered the public's opinion of me, which even today seems very high, I'm proud to say.

No, for me, it is the games you play at club level that really matter and the esteem you are held in by the supporters who pay to watch you week in, week out. In this respect, Joe Corrigan is one of the most highly regarded goalkeepers to have ever played for Manchester City and he was respected by opposing fans wherever he went – for me, that is the true mark of excellence.

Bert Trautmann, Valencia,
August 2008

Preface

I'd been toying with the idea of an autobiography for some time and actually began to write one a few years ago. For whatever reason, it was never finished and I shelved the idea.

In 2006, I was approached by David Clayton, editor of the official Manchester City magazine and James McCarroll, a publisher based in Ayr, to see if I was interested in getting my life story down on paper. We met in a Manchester hotel to discuss the project and I got on well with both David and James.

I soon signed a contract and over the next year or so, David began a series of interviews at my house, the results of which are in the remainder of this book and I hope you enjoy reading about my life in and out of football.

I expect the majority of people who buy this will be City fans, but I hope a few West Brom, Liverpool and Brighton supporters do, too. I had a wonderful playing career and while it hasn't all been sweetness and light – as you'll discover – I wouldn't change a single thing.

And more than forty years after making my debut for City, I'm still earning a living from the game as West Brom's goalkeeper coach, so I'm still enjoying my career and have no intentions of hanging my gloves up for a good while yet

I'd like to thank a small number of people for helping me in my career and without whom this book would not exist. Firstly, I'd like to thank my family but especially mum and dad for all the sacrifices they made and the support they gave. Thanks also to my sister Bernadette and brothers Paul, Kevin and Anthony.

For their unwavering support and advice over the years, thanks to Val's mum and dad, Brian and Rita, and to Uncle Thomas and all my aunties and uncles just for being there whenever I needed them. Special thanks to Bert Trautmann, one of my boyhood heroes, for the Foreword. He is a true gentleman.

In no particular order, all the following have helped me throughout my career and for that, I'm forever in their debt: Joe and Norah Mercer, Malcolm Allison, Harry Godwin, Harry Gregg, Ken Barnes, Tony Book, Roy Bailey, Freddie Griffiths, Trevor, Kath and Sue, and all the players I had the privilege to play alongside and against. Finally, I'm eternally grateful to Dr Leslie Huddlestone: without his help and expertise I would never have been able to walk again, let alone play football.

Joe Corrigan
Tytherington, June 2008

1

From Sale Moor to Sale Grammar

It was a long and eventful journey to arrive at a point in my career where I felt happy with my achievements in the game. There were times when I thought being a professional footballer was the best job in the world, and moments when I wondered whether all the pain was really worth it. To make it in the game you need ability, belief and determination, but luck plays a part, too. There's no magic formula that guarantees you are in the right place at the right time; it either happens or it doesn't. If it does, you have to make the most of your good fortune and work your backside off to make sure everything else falls into place. You also need to be thick-skinned and to battle on when the world is against you.

There were times when I almost lost faith in my own ability and thought about jacking it in. I've been called a 'fat bastard' by my own supporters, hammered by the press, bottled at Anfield and nicknamed Frankenstein by the United fans. But the good times far outweighed the bad and I look back on my playing career with great pride and affection and I hope others do, too.

We have to start somewhere so my story begins at St Mary's hospital, Manchester on 18 November 1948. My parents, Lily and Joe Corrigan, lived in Sale Moor to the south of the city centre and after I came kicking and screaming into the world they were informed by hospital staff that I was two inches longer than any other recorded birth at St Mary's. I'm not sure if that is true, but, if it was, my size was attracting attention, literally from day one. Nobody in our family batted an eyelid, however, because dad stood six feet two inches tall and his mother was only an inch or so shorter. The height definitely came from dad's side of the family because my mum's father was about five feet eight and quite stocky.

I was the first child and mum had to give up work to look after me while my dad was in the army as a full-time regular soldier. He was soon off to fight in the Korean War; not that I would have remembered as I was just seventeen months old when he shipped out. He was also forced to miss the birth of my sister Bernadette as he fought for his country. In fact, I didn't see much of him as a toddler, but I vividly recall one time he came home on leave, because he brought me back a US army jeep – a toy version, of course – and I spent countless hours pedalling down the alleyway between our house and the one next door pretending to be my dad patrolling the border that divided South and North Korea. There were no snipers, land mines or humidity to deal with in that alley, just constant drizzle, tin cans and the odd lump of dog dirt.

Thankfully, when the conflict ended in 1953, he returned home safely to our council house on Alderley Road to begin a new career as a lorry driver with a local firm. We lived on what was a prototype council estate, one of the first in Manchester; it was in effect an overspill made up largely of Roman Catholic families whose fathers had been away fighting in the war. It was a three-bedroom property, brand new, with many of the houses still unfinished when we first moved in. We even had an inside toilet – a real luxury – plus a warm seat in the winter. I would eventually share one bedroom with my three brothers, Paul, Kevin and Anthony, while my sister had her own room and my parents had the other. It might sound cramped, but we'd moved from my aunt's house, where there had been eight of us squeezed into a tiny three-bedroom house. We didn't have a great deal of money, but we survived and there was always food on the table and clothes on our back. We had plenty of support from relatives, many of whom lived close by, and my numerous aunts and uncles would muck in if we needed help. People were always there for you, especially family and friends, as the nation gradually found its feet in the years of austerity after the Second World War.

Family holidays were spent in Abergele or Rhyl with the odd trip to Blackpool thrown in. When we went to Wales, dad would hire a car and we'd cram in like sardines and be in raptures that we had a car for a whole week. We'd stay in a five-berth caravan and the weather could do its worst as far as we were concerned because there was always something to do. We had a wonderful time and I still have fantastic memories of those days. We'd go down to the beach, play football, fly a kite, or, if we were unlucky, catch sight of the rats running beneath the caravans.

By the age of six, I'd outgrown my toy jeep and football had taken over my life. However, there was a frightening period around that time which could have resulted in me never kicking a ball again. What had seemed like an innocuous bump on my knee, sustained during a kick-around at primary school, developed into something more sinister. In fact it was only through sheer chance that the condition I subsequently developed was successfully diagnosed.

My knee began to ache and I had a raging fever within a few days, and, when the doctor was called in to check on my progress, he immediately diagnosed a condition known as osteomyelitis, a difficult-to-treat infection of bone and bone marrow. The condition is progressive and results in inflammatory destruction of the bone, bone necrosis and new bone formation. It can also be fatal. Most doctors would probably have treated the knock and the fever as separate entities, but, by coincidence, my GP had suffered from the same infection and immediately recognised the symptoms. In fact, the illness had cost him his own leg, so he was well aware of the seriousness of the situation. I was rushed into Pendlebury children's hospital and immediately started on a course of antibiotics – a new form of medication at the time – and was soon on the way to a full recovery. My dad later told me that on the day I'd been admitted to hospital, he had to sign a consent form, which allowed the doctor to amputate the affected leg if my health worsened during the night. It would have done had I known that!

I owe everything to Dr Huddlestone, our family doctor. His 'reward' for saving me was to contract polio in his other leg and he was consigned to spend the rest of his days in a wheelchair. Sometimes life isn't fair, but I have him to thank for a normal childhood and I'm sure he took a lot of satisfaction from that. I left hospital in splints and wore them for six to eight weeks, but, as soon as I could, I was out kicking a ball around again. I now had a new appreciation of my health and the fact I was able to play normally again. How much that period would help me focus on achieving my goals I'm not sure, but the knowledge that the condition could return every seven years never left me – it still hasn't – and I was determined to make the most of life.

Every time I had an opportunity to play I did, and, unlike many goalkeepers, I actually started between the sticks rather than being lumped there because I couldn't play outfield. Discarded jumpers, trees or whatever we deemed to be goals; we loved it. They were wonderful, intoxicating days and I remember them with great affection.

At school I only ever wanted to play in nets, but as I was already considerably taller than most kids my age I was shoved up front as centre forward and that's the position I played regularly for my primary school, St Joseph's. Ironically, the lad who played in goal, John Birt, was fairly short and it angered me that I had to play the role of the lumbering forward because of my height when my real passion was to be the last line of defence.

Out of school was different and the small croft at the front of our house was our Maine Road, Old Trafford, or, if the occasion demanded, Wembley, as me and my mates enjoyed endless knockabouts on the small, tree-lined patch of ground. In truth, that's where I learned my trade, and I always played in goal. I'd even nip next door and get my pal Barbara Grange to come out and take shots at me when my other mates weren't around. My obsession with being the next Harry Gregg meant Barbera was inevitably nicknamed 'Mrs Gregg', though she didn't seem to mind. There were always plenty of lads on the estate who were up for a game and all of my brothers were into sport, too. My brother Kevin was an excellent footballer and should have gone on to play professionally, and Paul and Anthony both did well in cricket and rugby.

Such was my preoccupation with football that there was something close to disbelief when I passed my eleven-plus exam for Sale Grammar. Education wasn't regarded with the same importance as it is today because jobs were generally plentiful and if you didn't leave school with a plethora of qualifications it wasn't the end of the world because you'd always be able to earn a crust working in a factory of some sort. I think it did worry mum and dad that I was going to a grammar school because it was a big step for me and I'd have to stand on my own two feet. In addition, being from a strong religious background, the fact that it wasn't a Catholic school was also a concern for them. The fact is it gave me an insight into life away from the estate because many of the other kids were from middle-class families with bigger houses, bigger cars and bigger allowances. They lived different lives and it opened my eyes to what hard work could achieve.

There were very few Catholics at Sale Grammar and there were many times when we were treated poorly because of our faith, something I'd never experienced before. Along with a couple of Jewish kids we weren't allowed to go into assembly in the morning; if there were exams in the main hall, we'd have class assemblies and again we'd have to wait outside until they had finished. We were different and the powers-that-be at Sale couldn't have made that any clearer. On one occasion while we waited in the corridor, one of my Catholic pals cracked a joke that we all laughed at. When the assembly finished, we filed back in to our class to be told we had to write 500 lines for being 'irreverent'. I didn't even know what the word meant! My mum wasn't happy and while she said I should write 250 lines, she wrote a letter saying there had been a misunderstanding and that she felt I'd been sufficiently punished. I ended up being caned for not doing all of the lines. We just had to get on with it, and, although we were undoubtedly looked down upon and made to feel outcasts from time to time, there wasn't much we could do. It was just how things were in those days.

Whereas my size had never been an issue at primary school, it quickly caused me problems at Sale Grammar. Being an all-boys school at that time, and with most of my friends attending either a comprehensive or a secondary modern, I hardly knew anybody and was singled out as a threat by a few of the older boys, whom I already towered over. I was in detention within a few days for fighting with a lad who tried to pick on me. New kids were routinely subjected to an initiation ceremony, and, more often than not, that meant shoving your head down a toilet and having the water flushed over you. But I wasn't having any of that and ended up in a scrap with my would-be tormentor. I think that earned me a bit of respect because nobody ever tried it again.

In sporting terms Sale Grammar was a rugby-union-oriented school and playing football simply wasn't on the agenda; they saw it as the sport of the working classes and therefore frowned on it. I'd have to find other ways to get my fix in goals, but I played rugby to keep fit and quite enjoyed it for a while. I also represented the school at cross-country (even though I hated it with a passion), rugby, boxing and athletics, all of which helped stiffen my resolve and increase my stamina, attributes that would serve me well in later years. My boxing career would be deemed something approaching child cruelty in today's world because I was forced to fight boys two or three years older than I was due to my height and weight. I was too big for my own age group and the result was I got a few real hidings in the ring, but that, and playing as a second-row forward for the rugby team, proved an excellent grounding.

I wasn't afraid to go in where it hurt and I soon got used to taking knocks. I suppose I did feel a little differently going to a such a posh school and I think I was the only kid from our estate who went to Sale Grammar because most of my pals went to Norris Road secondary modern, just down the road from where we all lived. A couple went to Altrincham Grammar, and when we'd all meet up to play footie at the weekend there would plenty of good-natured ribbing and it wasn't unusual for one of my pals to call me a 'toffee-nosed bastard'.

The main thing was we all stuck together through thick and thin, and, whenever there was a rumble, the school you attended was the last thing on our minds. There'd be rival gangs we'd occasionally meet for a ruck and really big scraps took place on a piece of waste ground off Baguley Lane. Between our estate and the Wythenshawe council estate there were fields and a brook and we'd go up and play a match against the kids from Wythenshawe and it would always end up in a mass brawl – it was part and parcel of the way things were. I'd get involved in the odd scuffle, but no more than that, and I made sure I steered clear of those older lads who took things more seriously.

Things never got completely out of hand and serious crime was virtually unheard of on our estate at that time. It didn't do any harm that there was a policeman living near my house whom everyone respected. He'd talk to kids in the old-school style and though there were no doubt petty criminals operating in the neighbourhood, the worst offence I knew of was someone caught pinching apples. That's not to say I wasn't aware that there was a violent underbelly out there in the big, bad city, and, one afternoon I recall my dad coming home, battered and bruised from a fight with his brother Vince. He'd gone round because Vince's son, Thomas, had shot him in the leg with an air gun and a family argument had quickly developed into a fight.

Thomas was a legend in the Corrigan family. Built like the proverbial brick out house and as hard as nails, he commanded total respect from his peers. I remember he once saved a bullock from being slaughtered because he didn't like the idea of it being killed. He then walked it from

Smithfield Market in the city centre back to his local pub in Sale Moor. He tied it up at the bar and issued a warning that no one should touch the beast. Inevitably, the bull freed itself and proceeded to wreck the pub. Thomas had gone by that point but the police, who had – let's say – been interested in Thomas over the years, caught up with him and after locking him up, one officer goaded him about the jail sentence he could expect. Thomas reached through the bars and tore off the cop's entire upper uniform – at least, that's how legend has it. In later years he was attacked with a lump hammer in a nightclub – an attack that would have killed most men – and only his incredible strength saved him, though he's never been the same man since. But who would be?

So the gang culture and seedier side of life passed me by, for which I am eternally grateful. Besides, if I'd strayed off the straight and narrow, my parents, uncles or the local priests would soon have found out and put me back on the right track. I was more interested in sport than in defending the honour of our council estate. So much so, that, from the age of fourteen it was rugby in the mornings for the school, and, during the summer, cricket in the afternoon. During the winter months I'd play in goal for my uncle's local team, Sale FC, in the Altrincham and Sale open-age league, which was also great experience because I was a raw kid playing against enthusiastic blokes who were as hard as nails and decent players too. My first appearance for Sale was also rewarded with a bike from my dad, who was obviously proud that I was playing with the big boys. Not that my prized gift lasted too long; on one of my few trips on the gleaming new bike, I proudly parked it against the kerb out-side a local newsagent only to emerge as a bus pulled away leaving a mangled heap of metal on the road.

It is at this point that I have a confession to make. All City fans look away now and go straight to chapter two! Sale Moor was a staunch Manchester United area, and, with the Munich air disaster still fresh in the nation's memory, I too classed myself as a Red as a kid. It was the way things were in our area and I went along with it like everybody else. I recall my dad asking me if I was sure I supported United; I told him I thought so, because everybody else did. He said, 'well there's another team in Manchester, you know – Manchester City,' and he went on to tell me about 'the greatest keeper' he'd ever seen, Bert Trautmann, who played for City.

It was the first time City had entered my consciousness and I kept an eye out for any news about Trautmann from then on. I soon learned of another great City keeper, Frank Swift. It was clear that if any local club had a real tradition for goalkeepers, despite United having the great Harry Gregg, it was the Blues and not the Reds. It was an eye-opener and I developed a soft spot for City. I had to rely on snippets in the newspapers to keep track of the two Manchester giants as we didn't have a television and, even if we had, football was only on for a fraction of the time it is today. I had to make do with grainy images of Trautmann on the odd Pathe news bulletin at the cinema. My uncles would take me to the occasional match at Old Trafford to watch United and I'd take my brothers along to see the likes of Bobby Charlton and George Best, who were never less than entertaining. I was still a million miles away from being a Manchester City diehard, although that would soon change.

We lived in the same house as I progressed through Sale Grammar and it was always a happy home. Christmases were fun and, with five kids, a little manic for mum and dad. There was no room for pets, though dad came back from the pub one night with a mangy, flea-infested old dog after one shandy too many. His stay with us was to be a short one, but when it came to catching things, that pooch was right up there with any of the goalkeepers I admired. The dog would often come home with a live chicken – his own hot takeaway – and then present it to one of us in the kitchen. My dad would rescue the poor bird, usually mortally wounded, and (look away now if you're squeamish) pull its head off. The bird would run round the kitchen for a few moments in the classic, headless-chicken death throes before slumping on the floor, destined for the Corrigan cooking pot the following day. Oddly enough, images like those don't ever leave you. The dog was given his marching orders by my mum within a week and I never saw him again; the poor devil didn't even have a name.

For him, it really was a dog's life.

2

'One day this could all be yours'

Anyone watching my sporting progress through my high-school years might have surmised it was rugby, not football, that represented my future. I was captain of my house team and part of a side that remained unbeaten for four years. I was a second-row forward and I believe this helped shape me as a keeper because I had to jump during line-outs and was used to being on the ground grabbing the ball at people's feet and getting kicked and shoved around, which was all grist to the mill for an aspiring goalie.

I went along to rugby trials for Cheshire Boys and it was only a cracked bone in my arm that prevented me joining them. I can only speculate at what might have happened had I been taken on. One of my teammates – Michael Mulholland, a phenomenal all-round sportsman – went on to represent England schoolboys and another lad, Alan Graterix, became a boxing champion at schoolboy level and would later play rugby for Cheshire and England as a hooker. There were two others – Brian Labelle and Johnny Beswick – who also went on to do well in the sport.

Rugby was pretty much our sporting life at Sale Grammar and the only chance we had to play football was at break time, though our activities were frowned upon by the school authorities. It was a case of 'How can you play soccer on the hallowed turf of a rugby pitch or a cricket square?' We were dealing with institutionalised snobbery masquerading as enthusiasm for rugby but I suppose the school had to keep up its traditions, which I had no option but to accept. The school's sporting snobbery continued long after I'd left and I have to admit I felt a little disappointed that, despite being the only ex-pupil to go and become an England international, Sale Grammar never saw fit to put my name on the school honours board. Football didn't exist as far as the governors were concerned.

At home, I was taking on the extra duties that went hand-in-hand with being the eldest child, or big brother, depending on the situation. I was expected to muck in and look after my brothers and sister when necessary and – with dad at work all day and my mum having an evening job – that was quite often. But I never minded; it was part and parcel of being in a big family and my younger siblings were no trouble. I left school in 1965 with four O levels feeling I could have done a bit better in my exams but education wasn't thought of in the same way it is today. These days, leaving school, college or university with a clutch of paper qualifications is of paramount importance for youngsters. But in the early Sixties, you'd find a job without any difficulty and the skills you learned rarely relied on outstanding results in maths, English and geography – or Latin!

Manual work in factories was plentiful and apprenticeships taught you everything you needed to know about earning a living. If you applied for a job, you generally got it. It was an era when a careers advisor would drop into school and leave in the knowledge that a large proportion of the young people he'd seen wanted to be in engineering, apart, that is, from the dreamers who fantasised about being a footballer, movie star or perhaps even an astronaut. I was also a dreamer, but it didn't prevent me joining Allied Electrical Incorporated (AEI) in Trafford Park as an apprentice. At the induction interview, I was asked what I'd left school with and when it became clear that none of my qualifications were in metalwork or woodwork I was greeted with a kind of 'what are you doing here, then?' attitude. The truth is, I didn't know the answer to that question; it was just the way things were and working for an engineering giant like AEI was perfectly acceptable for any school leaver. After all, it started you off on what might well have been a job for life.

I joined the training school and was soon playing for the football team. The good thing was that rugby snobbery didn't exist in such a staunch working-class environment. On a less-positive note the factory was made up mostly of Manchester United fans; partly because of the location, partly because of the era. I enjoyed my time at AEI and I was soon mixing with some terrific characters, real salt-of-the-earth types who helped prepare me for the big, bad world outside. With the benefit of hindsight I now realise that I was a bit green and I made more than one fool's errand to the stores to collect, among other things, a long stand, a glass hammer or to have my hammer chucked. I'll spare you the results of such requests but I'm sure you can picture a young Joe Corrigan watching mystified as his hammer is thrown across the building and then slowly shrinking to the size of a mouse as the penny finally dropped.

Trafford Park was the biggest industrial area in Europe at the time, and there would be hordes of people arriving and leaving at the same time each day. It was, in many ways, a huge family. We were the worker ants and, for most of the blokes who worked there, it was their lot and it could well have been mine, too, had I not met certain individuals along the way. I was playing for AEI at centre-half in the week and Sale FC in goal at weekends and it was during an interdepartmental game at Trafford Park that my life began to fork down a different path.

One of the older guys I worked with was a former goalkeeper for the British Army. He'd been watching the AEI game and then saw me messing around in nets during a half-time break. He must have seen something in me that he liked because, a few days later, he asked whether I'd be interested in a trial at a league club. He was obviously well-connected locally and must have been scouting for clubs in the north-west for years. The league club he was offering a trial at was Manchester City. Not long after, he came back with a postcard from Harry Godwin, the chief scout at City, inviting me down for a game the following week.

I'd only been an apprentice for six weeks and I was now being presented with a chance of impressing City. I was still unsure whether I'd impressed as a centre-half or goalie. I travelled down to Maine Road by bus where I joined up with several apprentices waiting for a coach transfer to Cheadle Rovers' ground, where City's first team regularly trained. Tommy Booth, Kevin Glennon and Ray Hatton (whose son Ricky would, of course, become a world-champion boxer) were involved in the eleven-a-side match specifically arranged, I believe, to have a look at me in action. The club was looking for a youth-team keeper and I was surprised – and delighted – to be asked to keep goal, though I only realised I'd be the last line of defence when Harry Godwin threw me the green jersey in the dressing room. 'Put that on, son and let's get out there,' he said.

It didn't hit me at the time that the trial could change my life forever and so I played my usual game, without any nerves. I can't explain why I felt so calm, but although I didn't feel I had done particularly well, I must have done something right because I was signed on that evening as an amateur. The game flashed by and I can't recall that much of what I did, or didn't, do, but I enjoyed the experience and the standard was a lot higher than I'd been used to. I was excited about the prospect of following my dream and found it hard to concentrate on my job at AEI. Ironically, two weeks later, a letter arrived inviting me for a trial with Manchester United, but I turned them down. I had been given the chance I wanted and I wasn't about to jeopardise my prospects with City.

An integral part of signing an agreement with a professional club was giving up amateur football so I played my last game for Sale FC against a team called Dean's Blinds. We lost 10–1. After that, they were probably glad to see the back of me; I was just praying nobody from City was watching from the sidelines in case they changed their minds! A week later, I made my debut for City's A team against Bury. From there on I flitted between the A and B youth sides. I was still at AEI, but the football and work were beginning to clash. I was missing evening classes at work because I was training with City and it wasn't long before my bosses made it crystal clear they weren't happy with these absences during a vital part of my apprenticeship.

The truth was my heart was in football, not engineering, a point proved when I went up to collect my medal for winning an interdepartmental cup at a presentation in Stretford town hall. Manchester United defender Tony Dunne and his brother Pat Dunne, United's keeper, presented the medals to each player and as I went up, I said to Pat, 'By the way, I want your place at United.' I didn't smile, and must have cut an imposing figure, but, to his credit, Pat looked me right in the eye and said, 'Well you'll never get it, son.' He was right, of course, but considering what would happen across the city in future years, I'm more than happy I was proved wrong.

My desire to make a living in football meant that it wasn't long before the situation at AEI became untenable. So much so that, in February 1967, my dad told me I had to make a choice and take my chances. Fortunately, Malcolm Allison, City's enigmatic first-team coach, soon made it for me when he offered me a professional contract, which I was delighted to accept. In my first real meeting with the man who would have a dramatic influence on my career, I remember Malcolm saying: 'Look son, I want you to sign as a professional because I think you've got a chance. We've not got a third-team goalkeeper as such and I think you'll do OK. What do you think?'

It was a near two-year deal that would last until the end of the 1967/68 season: at £10 a week, it was £6 more than I'd been on at AEI. I was leaving behind a job for life and taking a hell of a gamble, but I'd never have forgiven myself if I'd not taken the plunge. I informed my employers of my decision and they tried to dissuade me, telling me I was throwing away a good, solid career, but nothing could have changed my mind. My family, Manchester United fanatics or not, were fully behind me and happy that I'd been given the chance of becoming a footballer. There'd be no more filling in at centre half before mucking around in nets at half-time; from now on it was goalkeeping all the way. I had around eighteen months to convince City that I was worth a longer deal, and, if I failed, it wouldn't be for the want of trying. My background in rugby had given me plenty of confidence to go in where it hurt and I wasn't afraid of flinging myself around, so the basics of goalkeeping were already there. But I realised there was a lot of fine tuning needed if I was to make real progress in the game.

I enjoyed being under Malcolm Allison's wing because he was a fantastic coach. No session was ever dull and he was always coming up with new techniques and methods to get the best out of us. Before my first training session with City, I recall Harry Godwin taking me out into the centre circle at Maine Road. The empty stadium was huge, with banks of terracing at three sides, and Harry just took a deep breath and said: 'One day, this could all be yours, son, if you put the work in.' I thought, 'yeah, sure'. I just wanted to get on with the session and show what I was made of. I was raw and enthusiastic and didn't want to waste a minute.

I was well aware of City's tradition for great keepers, with the likes of Frank Swift and Bert Trautmann, and there hadn't been a goalkeeper since who hadn't been compared with them. I knew the older fans had been weaned on two of the best in the world and they were big boots – or gloves – to fill. I was a young whippersnapper who nobody had heard of and many would have wondered who the hell I was. All I wanted to be was Joe Corrigan and to be given a fair crack of the whip like every-body else. I knew that if I could be even half as good as those two legends, I'd be a hell of a keeper. I'd be lying, however, if I didn't admit that the shadow of both men would become a huge millstone around my neck in the early years at Maine Road.

One of my first games for City was an FA Youth Cup tie at Anfield and it was also the first occasion that I recall Joe Mercer speaking to me. He told me that it was my job to keep the Liverpool defenders on the back foot by kicking the ball up field as quickly as I could. He reckoned they were too good to be allowed to settle and this was his method of making them turn and run back towards their own goal. We drew 2–2 and beat them 3–1 in the replay. Stan Bowles – a product of the youth team and a very talented lad who would go on to play for QPR and England – scored one of our goals that day, so the plan seemed to work. It was my first inkling that I was working under a guy who knew his stuff and liked to keep things simple.

Off the field there was no chance of me getting a big head; I knew my place in the scheme of things. It was a time when neither reserves nor apprentices were allowed near the first-team dressing room. Your job was to clean the boots, paint the walls, do odd jobs, something sadly lacking in today's game simply because it keeps your feet on the ground and makes you appreciate that life is hard on the outside. I became good pals with Tommy Booth, Ray Hatton and Tony Jackson and we'd kick off our games early because there were no floodlights at Cheadle and then, if the first team was at home, rush back to Maine Road to catch the match.

We'd make our way down the tunnel in the main stand to our seats, which were just behind the dugout. This was a time when the players' area wasn't nearly as secure as it is today and it was from here that the police would eject unruly supporters because it was the quickest route out of the ground. I remember one time, after City had beaten Everton, I was walking down the tunnel and there was an almighty scrap between Everton fans and the police taking place; it was mayhem. That was around 1968 when hooliganism was just beginning to affect the game and I can't recall ever seeing anything like that before and certainly not at such close quarters.

I was progressing fairly well in the youth teams and playing occas-ionally for the reserves. The three keepers ahead of me at that time were

Ken Mulhearn, Harry Dowd and Alan Ogley, but, when Alan joined Stockport County in 1967, it meant a step up the ladder for me. In some ways I was sorry to see him go because he was a brilliant reflex keeper and I felt I could have learned more from him. I remember watching him play for the first team – at home to Blackburn if memory serves – and he made an outstanding stop from close range. However, what most people didn't realise was that he was extremely short-sighted and had real problems with shots from distance. He wore contact lenses and after one particular save I noticed him crawling around the mud in the six-yard box after he'd cleared the ball; he was searching for a lens that had fallen out as the ball cannoned off his body. Needless to say, he couldn't find it and a shot from distance a few moments later flew past him into the net. Looking at the situation a little more selfishly, when Alan left it was one less goalie ahead of me in the queue for the first team. I'd have to impress Joe and Malcolm in the coming season if I was seriously to challenge Harry and Ken and earn myself a longer deal. The hard work was just beginning, but it was a challenge I relished.

3

Debut Disaster

I began the 1967/68 season, my first full campaign with City, full of optimism, though not expecting to play any first-team football. I just wanted to learn my trade in the reserves and in the A and the B teams, absorbing advice and observing the senior pros. How did they train? How did they prepare for games? How did they act away from football? There was a lot to learn, but it was very much a sink-or-swim situation. I had a lot of rough edges and needed to prove myself as quickly as possible if I was going to make a real go of being a professional footballer.

I'd not been at the club that long when there was a testimonial cricket game between City and United at Lancashire's Old Trafford ground. It was the first time two football teams had played there and I was asked to open the bowling. I had played cricket at school and had the build of a fast bowler so it seemed logical. The end result was probably the longest first over in history. I was trying too hard to impress the senior pros and bowled my first four balls wide. It was so bad that our wicket keeper, Harry Dowd, went and stood in the slips! In my mind I was Fred Trueman, but I was bowling more like Fred Flintstone. With my last ball, United's David Sadler, fed up with flapping at my wide deliveries, nicked my last ball and it went straight to Tony Book for what I believe is called a 'dolly catch'. Sadler traipsed off, crestfallen that he'd got out to my bowling, though not surprisingly I was taken out of the attack before I conceded a half-century of extras. There were twenty thousand people in the ground and it was an early introduction to the realities of life at such a big club.

Malcolm seemed to have a vested interest in my career and I could sense he had a real belief in my abilities. If he believed in you, he wanted to be proved right. He'd often take me for one-on-one coaching sessions and occasionally he would bring in experienced goalkeepers for a couple of hours of specialist coaching. Most afternoons, sometimes even on a Sunday, Malcolm would be out with me, firing in shots to improve my shot-stopping, crossing the ball from the wings and anything else he thought would help improve my game. He was so advanced in his thinking and methods and, long before anyone else made links to dietary requirements, he was recommending certain foods to eat that would prove beneficial and forever coming up with revolutionary methods and ideas to enhance our fitness. Considering he'd been an outfield player during his career, he was excellent with goalkeepers and it is testament to his brilliance as a coach that his talents weren't just confined to areas he knew about from playing there himself.

I was happy and thought I was doing well when, out of the blue, in October 1967, I was told the day before the first team were due to face second-division leaders Blackpool in a League Cup tie that I would be playing. I couldn't believe it. I hadn't even thought about playing for the senior side because I was the third-choice keeper and little more than a novice. I was eighteen and all of a sudden I was being thrown in at the deep end. The club had to order an extra-large keeper's jersey, because neither Harry Dowd's nor Ken Mulhearn's were big enough. On the plus side, with only twenty-four hours to go, I didn't have time to get nervous.

I remember travelling down to Maine Road to join up with the rest of the squad, but the rest of the pre-match period is little more than a blur. I was running on pure adrenalin, never more so than when I ran out at Maine Road for the very first time in front of a sizeable crowd of 28,000. I was confident, and, when I looked at the calibre of the players around me, I had to pinch myself that this was really happening. Mike Summerbee, Johnny Crossan, Alan Oakes, Colin Bell, Stan Horne. I was in exalted company and I needed to play my part.

With five minutes gone, Blackpool managed to get their first shot on target. A tame-enough effort that gave me the perfect chance to collect without too much fuss . . . only I didn't and instead watched the ball somehow squeeze through my legs and into the net. It was a disaster; my first touch in senior football on our own ground had resulted in a howler. I couldn't believe it. If a hole had opened up in the penalty area at that moment I'd happily have jumped in. Tony Book ran over, gave me a pat on the back and said, 'Come on lad, just get on with it.' That was typical of Skip, who would have done the same even if he hadn't been captain. He was a fatherly figure on the pitch and his maxim was to encourage, not to point the finger. I'm not sure how I would have reacted if someone had torn a strip off me at that point. It was a mistake and it was now confined to history and I had to get my head together quickly.

I'm not sure the City fans would have taken the same view. All they saw was a big lump of a teenager who had let in a simple shot in the first few minutes of his debut. Any thoughts of me being the next Frank Swift or the new Bert Trautmann had instantly evaporated, and it would take a long time before they trusted me to keep goal for their team. Although I didn't realise it at the time, the foundations had been laid for a rocky first few years with our supporters. Of course, experiences like that can make you stronger and it's all part of the steep learning curve you find yourself on. If you don't make mistakes you never improve.

I was thankful that I played reasonably well after my mistake and Mike Summerbee said to me at half-time that if we were still losing 1–0 with ten minutes to go, I should just launch the ball forward at every opportunity and one of the forwards would get a goal. That's what I did and, sure enough, Summerbee scored to take the tie to a replay. I was picked for that game, too, and was to meet up with the squad the following Saturday in Blackpool where Joe and Malcolm had taken the lads for a short break following a 2–0 win over Wolves. I was playing in the reserves in the afternoon so I had to travel up by train and, by the time I arrived at the hotel, everyone had gone out for the evening. Being a kid, I'd been told I had to go straight to bed, which I did. There would be plenty of opportunities for nights out if I ever became a first-team regular.

We trained on the beach on the Sunday and Monday leading up to the replay – I'd learn that Malcolm liked to take us to different environments to train – and it was while we were there that I first got to know Ken Barnes, then first-team trainer and one of the rummest blokes I've ever met. Ken was always up for a laugh, but on this occasion got a hefty dose of his own medicine. We were on the beach near our hotel, the Norbreck Hydro out towards Fleetwood, and with us was Joe Lancaster, a running coach. The night before we'd introduced Joe to the dubious delights of Advocaat, but, unbeknown to him, it was yellow shampoo with brandy in it. Joe drank several glasses and seemed to enjoy it, even if he was puzzled by the odd bubble coming out of his mouth.

But our practical jokes were far from over. As we jogged along the beach we approached the tramlines on the promenade and a few of the lads grabbed hold of Ken, stripped him naked and carried him to one of the pools of water on the beach. He was screaming at us, 'You bastards! Put me down you rotten bastards!' He was dunked in a pool and left by the shoreline. We jogged back to the hotel, but not before dispersing his clothing among the dunes. We watched from the hotel as he sprinted across the beach to the dunes and every now and then we'd see a head pop up as he searched for his togs. It was hysterical.

I played my second match against Blackpool, but this time I had a storming game, making an important save at 0–0 in a game we'd go on to win 2–0, which was a great relief. We drew Fulham in the next round and despite not being involved in league games I travelled with the squad hoping to keep my place. However, Harry Dowd had recovered from a hand injury and was selected instead. This time I did get to go out with the lads for my first real experience of the bright lights of London. It was an eye-opener and we had a few jars in a Soho nightclub called The Bag of Nails. But I was down about being left out and I chatted with a few of the senior pros who explained they'd all been in the same position at some point in their career, which helped a little. A few pints later and the world didn't seem so bad. I didn't play again that season and had to be content with continuing my education in the stiffs, though in all honesty, once you've had a taste of top-level football, it is the only place to be.

It had been an incredible first season and I was determined to witness its finale at St James' Park. Unless you've spent your life on planet Mars, I'm sure you will be familiar with the scenario: City needed a win to secure the title and to prevent Manchester United, who were playing at home to Sunderland, from pipping us at the post. Both Ray Hatton and I had played for the reserves on the Thursday before the match and we caught a bus to Newcastle on the Saturday. We had a train home already booked for, it was hoped, our triumphant return journey.

We stood in the paddock by the players' tunnel and watched the drama unfold at close quarters. It was a breathtaking match with City just edging a thrilling contest 4–3. We jumped over the barrier and ran down the tunnel after the teams had gone off and made our way to the dressing room, where the champagne was already flowing. We'd only been there a short time before Ray tugged my shirt and said we were going to miss our train. We legged it out of the ground, not knowing where we were headed, but eventually found the station only to be told the train had left five minutes earlier.

Marooned in Newcastle on a Saturday evening, we hadn't got a bloody clue what to do or where to go, so the only logical thing we could think of was to head back to the stadium and see if we could cadge a lift back to Manchester. Fortunately, on our arrival, half of Manchester was still at St James' Park and we had no trouble finding Joe and Malcolm and explaining what had happened. They told us not to worry and to hop on the bus with the rest of the lads, and that's how two wet-behind-the-ears kids got to share in the most momentous day in the club's history – from a unique point of view, you might say. We were told to sit at the back and coach Dave Ewing warned us to shut up and say nothing; we were happy to oblige.

We stopped in Harrogate on the way home and had a meal with the team. That's what City were all about in those days; there was a family atmosphere and we looked out for each other. There was no way we would have been allowed to make our own way home once they'd found out we were struggling for a lift, and, from then on, we were treated the same as the team that had just won the league championship. Champagne was available but we didn't really join in with the drinking. We were respectful of those around us, and besides, while we may have been City players, we hadn't contributed to winning the title.

It was a fabulous time to be at the club and Malcolm's advice ('you have got to train hard and the harder you train the more you will achieve') was clearly the only way forward. I had witnessed pure magic at Newcastle that day and it made me even more determined to be part of a winning Blues side. I vowed there and then to work until I dropped.

4

Learning from the Master

I found myself in something of an odd situation after we'd won the league. I was neither one thing nor the other and was in a strange limbo between first team, youth team and reserves. I didn't travel with the squad for the month-long tour of North America and I was now too old for the youth team. Ken Mulhearn was number one and Harry Dowd was the reserve-team keeper. There were no goalies on the bench back then, with only one substitute allowed, so I wondered when my chance would come to impress the management. I could train as hard as I wanted, but unless I could play matches it would be almost impossible to displace either Ken or Harry.

In fact, I'd all but convinced myself that the available berths would be taken and my short career at City would be over before it had really begun. So it was a huge relief when I was told by Malcolm that I was being offered a new twelve-month contract. I still didn't know where I'd be playing my football, but fortunately, an FA rule change came to my rescue. The Lancashire League A Division – once exclusively for youth-team players – had now become an open-age league. It meant that, if nothing else, I'd be able to play at least once a week.

I wasn't being paid much, but I didn't care. I had another year to prove myself and get myself up with the big earners. In previous years, two goalkeepers were pretty much all most clubs needed, but Harry's injury had forced Joe and Malcolm to reassess the situation. They didn't want to be in a position in which the alternative to the reserve keeper

was some untried kid from the youth team, especially as they'd be starting the season as defending champions and playing in Europe for the
first time.

The early part of the new campaign was a mix of Lancashire League
football and the odd reserve game. Malcolm, however, realised that I
needed to be playing at a more competitive level. Even he would have
found it hard to justify another contract if I'd still been third choice in
a year's time. I was twenty and needed to be playing regular first-team
football in order to put pressure on Ken and Harry, and, if it wasn't at
City, it would have to be somewhere else.

Then, in October 1968, I got the break I had been looking for. Harry
Gregg, the legendary former Manchester United goalkeeper and my
hero as a kid, had become manager of third division Shrewsbury Town.
His only experienced goalie was John Phillips, for whom he had no
cover. He rang up Malcolm and, having seen me play youth-team football not long before, asked if he could take me on loan to Gay Meadow.
It was the perfect opportunity to stretch myself and show what I could
do and, of course, I'd have the ideal coach in Gregg, a keeper I'd always
admired. As commuting from Manchester to Shrewsbury was out of the
question, it meant I'd be leaving home for the first time. It would also
give me a taste of life further down the leagues. In short, if things didn't
work out at City, or if I didn't make them happen, that level could well
be my future whether I liked it or not. What I didn't realise at the time
was the huge impact my time with Shrewsbury would have on my life,
both personally and professionally. I couldn't wait to get started and
travelled to Shropshire desperate to begin my loan spell and perhaps
impress enough to get one or two games under my belt. Whatever happened, I was determined to make the most of my time under Harry's
watchful eye and to absorb his advice. I would be learning from the
master.

Harry had been my inspiration to become a keeper in the first place,
but this was the first time I'd actually met the great man face-to-face.
His first words to me were, 'Jesus Christ! I had no idea you were as big
as you are, lad.' He sat me down and said, 'I'm going to make you a
goalkeeper, son.' I felt like pinching myself. We then had a long chat and
he told me about his playing days and the basics he'd learned at an early
age playing for Manchester United and the Busby Babes and beyond.

He told me that I needed to be brave and strong and not allow myself to be pushed around. As an example, he told me about the time he was playing at Anfield and Ronnie Yates whacked him as a corner came over. The next time Liverpool had a corner, Harry retrieved the heel of a hobnail boot that had been chucked at him earlier in the game from behind his goal. As the corner was about to be taken he showed the heel, which had nails sticking out, to Yates and said, 'This is for you, big man.' Yates slowly turned around and jogged out of the box, clearly unsettled by the antics of this wild Irishman. There was another time Harry bit an attacker's leg when he'd fallen on top of him and the lad screamed in agony. I wasn't in any doubt that Gregg was as hard as nails but he was also an incredibly brave man as his actions at the 1958 Munich air disaster – which caused the tragic deaths of so many of the Busby Babes – clearly illustrated. Just after the crash it is well documented that he went back to the plane, by this time a blazing inferno, to rescue survivors. As well as Bobby Charlton and other teammates he pulled a baby girl and her mother to safety. It is little wonder that he was later dubbed the Hero of Munich. So when somebody with his background and standing in the game told you what he expected, you listened.

'Give me what I want – 100 per cent effort – and I'll be happy to work with you,' was Harry's simple maxim. Malcolm had instilled a work ethic in me already, but Harry took it to the next level: total goal-keeping. Without his guidance, I might never have made it.

In my first game for Shrewsbury reserves against Southport, I was clattered by a gnarly old centre-forward, and, although he didn't score, it knocked the wind out of me. At half-time, Harry looked pissed off and said: 'Look son, if you're not prepared to do what I want you to do and you don't use your weight and size to protect yourself and be a man, I'll send you back tomorrow morning. It's your call.' Those words rat-tled me in exactly the way he'd hoped, and, when the opportunity arose, I clattered the centre forward back. That little vignette, I have no doubt, started my career in earnest. Years later, Harry would claim that I never looked back after that night; I agree with him, even though there would be many trials and tribulations ahead.

I quickly adjusted to life at Shrewsbury. At Maine Road, everything was done for us and life was pretty cushy; a complete contrast to Gay Meadow where we had to do most things ourselves. The training ground was owned by the Royal Horticultural Society, with a wooden hut as our changing rooms. We'd leave our kit in the hut overnight, caked in mud, and if you stood it in a corner, it'd be there the following morning, untouched and ready for the next session until it was finally washed after training on a Friday. I'd been brought in purely as cover and would play the majority of my games in the Northern Floodlit League, turning out at a succession of obscure football outposts against older players in the dying embers of their careers. Nevertheless, it was the perfect grounding and I'd won Harry's respect; it was manna from heaven.

Harry's coaching wasn't confined to the training ground. We'd spend hours talking; him the learned scholar, me the eager student. We went over different scenarios and what was best to do or not to do in each situation. Malcolm had worked tirelessly with me at City, but he realised I needed more and his foresight in loaning me out would one day be of great benefit to Manchester City. Alf Wood – a centre half at Shrewsbury, who'd once played for City – taught me how to take a pummelling during crossing sessions. He was as hard as nails and as daft as a brush, but his no-holds-barred challenges when I went to pluck the ball out of the air helped condition me for the battering that was an integral part of life as a top keeper. I may have been left covered in bruises after half an hour at close quarters with Alf, but it was exactly what I needed.

It was almost unheard of to go out on loan in those days, but, once again, Malcolm was ahead of the pack. In fact it wouldn't surprise me if he'd been one of the pioneers of the loaning system. In later years I would learn that Joe Mercer was planning to release me at the end of the 1968/69 campaign so this had perhaps been Malcolm's last throw of the dice. After a few weeks under Harry's wing, I'd already moved on to the next level of goalkeeping. I'd get an hour with him after each training session and I became a human sponge for that period of time. Some people say that Malcolm made me and that I was a manufactured keeper, but I don't believe that it's possible to create a goalkeeper. You are either a keeper or you are not and it all comes down to two factors: your innate ability and how you adapt to the coaching. You need to be strong and brave to survive and it was Harry Gregg who honed my natural instincts. He was perhaps the biggest single influence on my career, though without Malcolm's belief, I'd have never got the opportunity to learn from a man who, for me, had no peers.

I was happy in my digs in the town and enjoying my football and all I needed to top things off was a run in the first team with Shrewsbury. But it never happened. John Phillips remained injury free and I never made an appearance for them during my three-month stay, which was a shame as I'd have loved to have shown Harry how much of his coaching I'd absorbed. Shrewsbury were struggling and I was playing out of my skin in the reserves, but I could understand Harry not dropping Phillips, who was a great young goalkeeper. If he had, it would have been tantamount to saying his keeper was to blame for their plight, which wasn't the case at all. At least Malcolm had been present at about three-quarters of the reserve games I played in and I greatly appreciated his interest in my progress. It would have been easy for him to ship me out and forget about me, but that wasn't his style; Malcolm saw things through to the end and if something failed, it wouldn't be for the want of trying.

I was finally recalled to City in January 1969, following Ken Mulhearn's cartilage operation. I was raring to go because I'd learned so much and wanted to show everyone how much I'd come on. Malcolm told me he was disappointed Harry hadn't given me a chance in the first team, but I still felt the main aims of the move had been fulfilled. Today, when Premiership clubs loan players to lower-league sides, it's almost mandatory that they play if they are fit. I'd experienced a different way of life to the one I'd known, branched out on my own, met my future wife Val and learned a hell of a lot about goalkeeping.

I'd better rewind slightly at this point now that I've mentioned the lady I was destined spend the rest of my life with. It's funny how fate occasionally nudges you down certain paths. In theory, I should never have met Val, but a sequence of events over the course of a couple of days, ensured that I did and, forty years on, we're still happily married.

I'd been due to play for Shewsbury reserves on the Saturday, but the game was called off on the Friday before due to a heavy snowfall. Three of the Shrewsbury lads I was friendly with – John and Terry Garbet and Tony Loskor – were going out for a pint and John called me and asked me to join them. There was a dance being held in a place called Pontesbury; I didn't have any plans and was happy to tag along. We drove to a pub called the Nag's Head before we went to the dance and while we were there I got chatting to a local girl at the bar. We got along fairly well but

I thought no more of it. As we were leaving, two girls came out and I thought one of them was the girl I'd been talking to. We offered them a lift, which they accepted, and after we'd all squeezed in, I realised it wasn't the girl I'd chatted with at all; it was a girl called Val and her aunt, although her aunt was actually younger than she was.

We went to the dance and she left about midnight, when her dad turned up to take her home. But we had really hit it off and agreed to go out together a few days later and things moved on from there. I told Val I was a carpenter – with a name like Joseph it was the first thing that popped into my mind – but it went straight over her head. She wasn't into football so saying that I was Shrewsbury Town's reserve goalie just didn't sound that impressive. When I eventually told her what I did for a living, I don't think she realised what dating a professional footballer might entail and I'm not sure I did at that point, either. So, that's our story – in brief – and now back to football!

I soon settled back in at Maine Road and I started taking the train down to see Val whenever I got the opportunity. I was happy with life, although I knew I had to break into City's senior side before the end of the season. If I failed to make the breakthrough, the club quite understandably would have no reason to offer me another deal. It would come down to whether or not I was viewed as the future number one because neither Ken nor Harry Dowd showed any desire to move on and they were both solid keepers. There was a brief period when I was promoted to number two while Ken was injured and I was playing regular reserve-team football. There was one occasion, however, that almost proved disastrous. Away to Sheffield United, I'd chatted beforehand with Tony Coleman and he told me he'd make himself available on the wing if I was looking for a quick throw-out. During the game, the ball came over; I collected it and made to throw it out to TC, but he'd drifted in from the touchline, which meant I had to stop myself in mid-flow and keep hold of the ball. The momentum of the throwing action meant the ball squirmed out of my hand as I spun around and it dropped on the line. Had the pitch not been so muddy, it would have ended up in the back of the net, but it stuck there and I dived on it, mightily relieved. Gary Sprake of Leeds wasn't so lucky later that same season, when he did the same thing in front of the Kop; unfortunately for him there was no mud to stop the ball bouncing into the empty net for a comical own goal. I'd been lucky to get away with it and I chalked it up to experience. If it had gone in, I'm not sure I could have regained the confidence of Joe and Malcolm, or my own.

Then, on 11 March 1969, just two months after my return, Harry Dowd picked up an injury. As Ken had been ruled out for the season with a bad knee injury, I was told I'd be making my league debut away to Ipswich. It was my first involvement since playing against Blackpool eighteen months before and I knew I had to seize the opportunity – with both hands, to coin a phrase.

Before the game I received a telegram from Harry Gregg. It read: 'You are the biggest and the best – now stay in.' That gesture was typical of Harry and it meant a hell of a lot to me. The pressure was off as regards retaining the league title; we were so far off the pace we could never have caught the leading pack, but I enjoyed the game even though we lost 2–1. Harry recovered but I played against Nottingham Forest two games later and, if the clippings I've kept of that game are to be believed, played a blinder in the course of a 1–0 defeat.

With nothing to play for in the league, I was obviously being blooded at first-team level to see if I had what it took. My next game was a tough test for any keeper – away to Leeds United at Elland Road. Just before kick-off Malcolm told me that centre half Jack Charlton was a problem I'd have to deal with on crosses and I shouldn't expect anyone to bail me out. Big Jack had a reputation for roughing up keepers, but Malcolm reckoned our defenders needed to concentrate on other things and that I had to look after myself, which was fair enough. I took a bit of a buffeting, but handled myself well. I was up for the challenge and there is no doubt all those sessions with Alf Wood were starting to pay off. Besides, I was used to the physical side of the game from my days as a rugby player and, let's face it, if I couldn't look after myself with my size and weight, I had a real problem. Though we lost the match, I edged my duel with Big Jack and felt I'd done enough to merit a sustained run in the first team. I couldn't believe the papers the next day, with more than one asking whether City had another Frank Swift on their hands. To be even mentioned in the same breath as Swifty was an incredible honour.

I was even on stand-by for the 1969 FA Cup final against Leicester City and travelled down with the team by train, not daring to dream of actually playing. Joe Mercer had said in the press that there was no chance of me replacing Harry Dowd and I understood that, though you could never be totally sure. I enjoyed the build-up to the match, but ultimately I wasn't called on. It was still a wonderful experience for a young kid and a fantastic fillip to beat Leicester 1–0, especially after having performed so indifferently in the league. We went to the Café Royal after the match and it was there that I saw left winger Tony Coleman looking as depressed as I'd ever seen anybody in my life. He was in the toilet and he reckoned he'd played badly during the final, letting the club and himself down. We'd all had a few drinks and that can stir different emotions in different people but TC, the great enigma, was crestfallen, which was a shame because he was a hell of a player. 'I've just sold my winner's medal,' he told me solemnly. I couldn't believe it because, as a youngster, winning an FA Cup final was the stuff dreams were made of, yet here was a man who looked like his world had ended and clearly didn't believe he had earned the right to own a winner's medal. It was bizarre. Whether he really had sold it, I don't know, but it was an odd thing to say if he hadn't. TC was a law unto himself and you learned to expect the unexpected from him.

Malcolm later got hold of me before the first team went out on a bender and stuffed £80 in my pocket so that the younger lads and fringe players could have their own celebrations in our Finsbury Park hotel. It was typical of him to remember those who had not played and a group of us – including Tony Jackson, Graham Howell, Dave Cunliffe, Ray Hatton and Ronnie Healey – had a great night. We'd been through a lot together, coming through the ranks to the brink of the senior side and we stuck together like brothers.

We had another reception in Manchester after our homecoming and it was the first time that I'd ended up completely paralytic while I'd been with City. Neil Young, Harry Dowd and George Heslop were in close attendance during the evening, which took place at the Ritz in the city centre. I was just happy that I'd been invited and that evening Dowdy and George introduced me to the dubious pleasures of Bacardi and Coke. It would be my first and last meeting with that particular concoction; I've never touched the stuff since and can't even stand the smell of it now, but that night I guzzled more than I could handle. As I knocked them back, the senior pros kept a close eye on me, and, at the end of the night, Dowdy and his wife dropped me home in a taxi and made sure I was okay.

That's how we did things; we looked out for one another and, when necessary, closed ranks.

It was a great time to be part of the club. I had the opportunity to become first choice for City and all I had to do was make sure I didn't screw things up when I got the chance.

5

Glory Daze

With four league games and two League Cup ties under my belt in two years, it was make or break time at the end of the 1968/69 season. I had no inkling at all what Joe and Malcolm's intentions were regarding my future and if they'd called me into the office and said to me 'Sorry, son,' I'd have been devastated, though not entirely surprised. As it turned out, I'd done more than enough to earn their trust, as the 1969/70 campaign would prove. I signed a new deal, still expecting to be third in line for the first team when Ken and Harry were fully fit. That's not to say I didn't have belief in my ability, it's just the way things seemed likely to go, or at least that's how I saw it. Instead, I was elevated to first-choice keeper on merit for the start of the new season and there was nobody more surprised than me.

The first clue I had about my imminent promotion came when I was selected to play in the Charity Shield match against Leeds United at Elland Road. It was a pleasant surprise and a great experience to once again face the likes of Billy Bremner and Allan Clarke. We lost 2–1 in front of almost 40,000 fans and I awaited the team sheet for the opening league game of the season against Sheffield Wednesday with great antici-pation. There was a definite shift towards bringing through younger players and this would be the season when Ian Bowyer, Tommy Booth, Tony Towers and I were all given the chance to shine.

When I was handed the number-one jersey for the league curtain-raiser, I was determined to keep it for as long as I was a Manchester City player. I was still relatively unproven at the highest level and I knew deep down that it was Malcolm's call to play me. I was desperate to replay the faith he'd shown in me.

In my second game, we were 2–1 up at Liverpool with about five minutes remaining, but they came back to win 3–2 with two late goals, neither of which, I'm happy to add, I could have done much about. That game was the beginning of a relationship with the Liverpool fans that would last for more than thirty years and I suppose it all began when someone threw a meat pie at me as I ran towards the Kop. The pie landed in my nets and I walked straight to it, took a bite and threw it back into the crowd. The Scousers loved that and roared their approval. They never forgot that moment and there was a mutual affection between us from then on. It was also the start of numerous renditions of, 'Who ate all the pies?' On this occasion, it had the ring of truth. There was, of course, an element of truth regarding the pies chant. I knew I was over-weight at about fifteen-and-a-half stones and needed to shed a few pounds, but things were going well and I suppose I just carried on the way I was. Why fix something that didn't seem broken?

The first few weeks of the season suggested we wouldn't be challeng-ing for the title again. I was coming up against top strikers every week, and, in my first Manchester derby, I recall diving to collect the ball, and, as I did, feeling pain shoot down the back of my hand. I looked up to see Denis Law trotting away having left his foot in. He looked back over his shoulder and said, 'Welcome to the first division, son.' I just got up, brushed myself off and got on with it. You had to look after yourself and if they could see what they were doing got to you, it was a lost cause. We won that game 4–0, not a bad way to start your derby career. Bear in mind that I came from a family of Reds, so, as you can imagine, I took a bit of stick that weekend. I didn't care; I was on cloud nine. Even though I'd been a United fan as a kid those days were long gone and thrashing them that day couldn't have been any sweeter.

In November 1969, I was informed I'd been called into the England under-twenty-three squad for the game against Russia at Old Trafford. It was a dream come true to represent my country, aged twenty, with only a handful of first-team appearances under my belt. I was delighted to be called up as a replacement for the injured Peter Shilton and it was the great Sir Alf Ramsay who was the manager, another terrific honour for me. John Hurst and Joe Royle of Everton were playing as well as Emlyn Hughes, David Nish, Brian Kidd and Peter Osgood. I was honoured to be in such talented company. I made sure I kept my shirt and later gave it to my dad to do whatever he wanted with it.

I didn't have a close relationship with the City fans at this time. It was still a getting-to-know-you period and no bond had yet been forged. One of the lads who had broken through to the first team around the same time as me was Ian Bowyer. Ian was a promising young forward who knew where the back of the net was and he would finish the campaign as second-top scorer in the league behind Franny Lee, not a bad achievement for a first season. It was one that should have made him a firm favourite with the City fans, but, for some reason, things just went from bad to worse in that relationship. He was a good finisher and terrific in the air and, although he may not have been the most elegant footballer, he was certainly effective. Nevertheless, for some reason, the supporters never took to him and, in time, he became a scapegoat. Of course, I would have a rough time, too, but that was in the future.

I think the odds were against Ian from day one because we had so many crowd favourites in the team; players of genuine international class like Colin Bell, Franny Lee and Mike Summerbee. When things were going badly – and we were having a very average season – there was no way the fans were going to turn on players of that calibre. They would vent their frustration on players they had no history with – no bond to break – and that meant the youngsters coming through had to tread very carefully. The team was packed with skilful players and then all of a sudden there is a big, raw lad in goals and a big, raw lad up front. We were both doing our job, but were the target for some unfair criticism in the newspapers. The bad press seeped on to the terraces, particularly in Ian's case. We were told not to read the papers but you did, of course. We were kids and it was novel to read someone else's supposedly unbiased opinion on how you were performing – or not as the case might be. It hurt, but you had to prove the knockers wrong.

I was enjoying our European run and my first-ever game in the Cup Winners Cup was in Spain against Atletico Bilbao. We drew three-all with a couple of late goals leaving us in pole position for the second leg. The crowd were right on top of us that night and it was an intimidating atmosphere. The Spanish fans were drinking wine and shouting abuse from the banks of terraces. The game also introduced me to the wily ways of players from the Continent. On one occasion I had the ball in my arms ready for a kick out when someone snuck up from behind and tapped the ball out of my grasp before rolling it home. Fortunately, the ref saw it and the next time I got the ball I defiantly clutched it close to my chest, a practice I would adopt for the rest of my career.

I'd been violently sick before the game, despite having my usual pre-match meal of steak. I think Tommy Booth was rough, too, but it could have been a routine stomach bug. I made it through the game okay and afterwards felt good enough to join the rest of the squad for a meal in our hotel. There were a number of City fans staying in the same hotel and they were enjoying themselves without imposing on us. The drinks were flowing, but, before we could down too many, Dave Ewing and Johnny Hart ordered my roommate, Ian Bowyer, and I to bed. We were kids and did as we were told. Some of the senior players had peeled off to have their own drinking session elsewhere in the hotel, but Ian and I dutifully turned in for the night. I was half asleep when I heard loud noises coming from the staircase. It sounded like someone was the worse for wear and Ian asked me what I thought the racket was. I got up and peeked outside the door just as this guy, whom I recognised as a City supporter, was climbing the stairs. He'd had a few and was causing an almighty commotion on what I assumed was the way back to his room.

'Is there a problem?' I asked him.

'I lost my key,' he slurred in reply, dangling what was probably the hotel's spare key. I could see that his room number was just down the corridor from us and, because he was staggering so badly, I offered to help. He nodded and I walked him along the corridor. As we got to his door, right out of the blue, he turned and punched me in the stomach. Without thinking, I retaliated and gave him a crack on the jaw. His head hit the door and he went out like a light. I could see that something didn't look right around his cheek and eye and I feared I might have broken something, or, worse still, killed him. I ran back to my room and told Ian to fetch Dave Ewing quickly.

Dave came upstairs at a rate of knots and took one look at the guy before running off to find the club doctor. The next thing, all hell broke loose and I was dragged into my room where Dave gave me the third degree. Why had he hit me? Why had I reacted? It had been an instinctive reaction, nothing more, but he quite rightly tore a strip off me because I'd acted foolishly. Even though I was in the wrong, everyone quickly closed ranks around me, but not before Franny Lee burst into my room to give me another dressing down. 'You fucking idiot,' he shouted, before firing a verbal volley that I couldn't respond to. He was right and he was a senior pro; I just had to let him get on with his rant, even though he wasn't fully aware of the circumstances.

It shouldn't have happened, but then we shouldn't have had fans staying in our hotel. The club later realised as much and changed the procedures with regard to accommodation. I think City had to pay to keep the incident out of the papers, but it certainly taught me a lesson I would never forget. The guy I hit had a depressed fracture of the cheek-bone, which I wasn't proud of, and I apologised to him and his family at a later date.

On the pitch, we saw off Bilboa 3–0 in the second leg and then comfortably dispatched SK Lierse of Belgium in the next round, 7–0 on aggregate. By December we had also made it through to the semi-final of the League Cup so while things were going well in the cup competitions our league form was patchy at best. For me, it almost didn't matter a jot as I came perilously close to losing my life in a car crash. The fact that I survived and could still play football was a minor miracle.

I'd picked up a groin strain in the home leg against Lierse and was doubtful for the league match with Leeds three days later. On a whim, I travelled up to Shrewsbury on the Thursday in my new Cortina GT Mangoletsi conversion and decided to stay over. It snowed heavily while I was there, and, needing to get back to Maine Road for treatment, I prepared to travel home early on Friday morning, just in case the weather worsened. The car wasn't having any of it, unfortunately, and Val's dad towed me to a garage to get it started. As soon as it was fixed, I paid the mechanic, checked my watch and drove off like a bat out of hell. Approaching Whitchurch, I was still going like the clappers but was at least thirty miles from Maine Road. To make matters worse, I then got stuck behind a slow-moving lorry. There was a long, open stretch of road beyond the truck and with nothing coming in the other direction, I put my foot down in an effort to make up a little time. I had just overtaken the truck when I drove over a patch of black ice. My car spun out of control and then rolled over several times before coming to rest on the grass verge.

I had been thrown about like a sock in a tumble dryer, but I maintain to this day that had I been wearing a seat belt – it wasn't compulsory in those days – I would have been killed instantly. I lay stunned for a moment just staring at the gear stick, trying to work out what had happened and where I was. The roof had been flattened to such an extent that I felt like a sardine. Finally, my survival instincts kicked in. I knew I had to get out quickly and so kicked the door open and scrambled onto the grass. The lorry driver I had passed an instant before had pulled over and was walking towards me with a look of disbelief on his face. He was amazed that anyone could have survived such a devastating crash. 'How the hell did you get out of that?' he asked.

I was in shock and couldn't give him an answer. In any event there was no satisfactory explanation; it had been a miraculous escape. He drove me to a local hospital to get checked over, but nobody would have ever guessed what had just happened to me. The doctor told me I was physically fine and after I'd informed the police and managed to get a lift back home, I eventually turned up at Maine Road and was hauled in front of Joe and Malcolm, who read me the Riot Act. I'd missed my treatment, was about three hours late and there would be no way I could play against Leeds the next day, fit or not.

Later on, I went to see my mum in hospital where she was recovering from a minor operation. She looked at me as I walked up to her bed and her first words to me were: 'Something's happened to you today, Joe, hasn't it?' I asked why she had said that and she told me it was because she could see I was in shock; she was right, of course. The whole episode taught me a valuable lesson: always go home the day before training and always avoid the need for excessive speed unless it's an emergency. I could have ended up in a wheelchair or even dead and for what? Whenever I went back to Shrewsbury after that, I took a different route or, preferably, travelled by train.

From December 1969 through to the end of the season, I experienced more highs and lows than most footballers have in an entire career. It was hard to keep pace: one moment I was celebrating with the rest of the lads as we booked another major final at Wembley and moved smoothly through the rounds in the European Cup Winners Cup; the next I was being hammered by teammates and supporters for lapses in concentration that threatened my place in the side and my future at the club.

After seeing off Manchester United in the League Cup semi-final we faced West Brom in the final and I looked forward to my first Wembley final in my debut season. Our league form was very inconsistent and we were going from the sublime (a 4–0 win at West Ham) to the ridiculous (nine games without a win thereafter). We were reinforcing the 'typical City' tag and during that winless streak we played away to Coventry City, when my poor performance would lead to me being dropped for the first time that season. We were 1–0 down and I came out for a cross I had no chance of collecting. I dropped the ball, presenting Coventry with a simple chance to make it 2–0. Malcolm had instilled in me that, with my size, I should make every ball that came within range of our penalty area mine. I admit I might have taken that advice a little too literally on occasion and this was one of them.

Following that gaffe Tommy Booth offered an excellent piece of advice. He said: 'Why do you keep coming out for balls that aren't yours, Joe? Who is going to beat you with a header from the edge of the box? Let us deal with crosses like that and you concentrate on the rest.' It made sense, but I couldn't rewind time so would have to take it on the chin and learn from the various bollockings I took. I got a grilling from Mike Summerbee, who wasn't impressed by my efforts, and other members of the team also lambasted me. We lost 3–0 and I was out of the side for the next few games, not sure exactly when I'd be back in favour. With a Wembley final just around the corner, the timing could not have been worse.

There were also problems off the field. I wasn't eating the right food in the right quantities nor was I training as hard as I should have been. I'd gone with the flow and because things were going my way I had let things slip. It was my first real crisis as a pro and I would be monitored closely to see how I reacted. It was all part of the learning process, but around this time there were snippets in the press referring to me as 'fatty' and suchlike. In my naivety I walked into a media trap by agreeing to be interviewed by the *Daily Express* and then to be pictured on a pair of scales in my mum's front room. I shouldn't have done it because it was inviting trouble. I weighed in at fifteen stones six pounds and I had completely underestimated the coverage I'd receive in the national press. We were due to play Burnley a few days later at Turf Moor and I knew I'd be a target for their fans, who were unforgiving at the best of times. I asked Malcolm if I could be left out and he replied angrily: 'Don't be so fucking stupid, man. Of course you're playing, whether you like it or not. You're a professional footballer so just get on with it.'

He was right and no doubt he was teaching me a lesson about airing my views in public. It was my bed and I had to lie in it and tuck myself in, too. We lost the game and, as expected, I took some awful stick from the Burnley fans – 'you fat bastard!' was one of the more printable chants. I admit that it hurt me, but I tried not to let it show because, if I had, I probably would never have wanted to play again. I learned from it and from then on worked my backside off to lose weight.

Ken Mulhearn was back in the box seat, but while things might not have been going so well on the pitch, off it I had my own big match planned: my wedding day. Val and I had decided to get married at the end of February 1970 because there was an end-of-season tour to Australia planned for May and it was agreed that it would be best for my career if I was on the plane with the rest of the squad instead of on a plane with Val heading for our honeymoon. The team hadn't won while I'd been dropped, but there was no indication that I'd be back in the side any-time soon. Then, on the eve of our nuptials, Joe Mercer called me into his office. He told me that he wouldn't be able to make my wedding, but then said I would be back in the side for the weekend trip to Wolves. With the League Cup final just a fortnight away, it was the best wedding present Joe could have given me and I told him as much. I was being given another chance and, from that day on, I'd never assume my posi-tion was safe and always check the team-sheet on the eve of each match. That maxim wouldn't change until the day I left the club in 1983.

On the eve of the League Cup final, against West Brom, we had a huge game to play in the European Cup Winners Cup quarter-final, first leg, and we flew out to Portugal to take on Academica de Coimbra, leaving with a hard-fought 0–0 draw. It was just three days before we took on the Baggies and we were due to fly to London the next day and stay until after the final. Our flight back to England, however, was diverted to Birmingham due to heavy snow in the capital and we had to get a coach down to our London hotel, costing us a day's training. After a session on Friday morning, Arthur Mann, a good mate of mine, came along with me to get a haircut and while we were in the barber's a photographer took an opportunistic picture, not that we were particularly bothered. A cartoon featuring the two of us appeared later with a reference to the state of the Wembley pitch, which I thought was odd because Wembley usually resembled a bowling green.

The next day, we travelled to Wembley by coach and I did my utmost to take it all in. I was determined not to let a moment of the day pass me by and it was amazing watching the people swarming towards the Twin Towers. There must have been 40,000 fans from each side in London that day. I tried to act as though everything was normal but inside the adrenalin was pumping and the anticipation was building. As we got off the coach, Malcolm took me to one side and said he wanted a word. 'What have I done now?' I asked, fearing the worst. As the other lads made their way to the changing rooms Malcolm said:

'That's the tunnel, go out and stand in the middle of the pitch.'

'Why? I need to get changed,' I replied.

'Do as you're told son. Don't argue. Just go and do it.'

So I set off down the tunnel towards the pitch. I could feel something tangible as I neared the mouth – some say it's like a curtain that can make or break you – but I could definitely feel something. I walked out to the centre circle and it was no more than a muddy, sticky, cow patch – a 'pig of a pitch' as Joe Mercer aptly described it afterwards. It was, I believe, the day after the Horse of the Year show. Could you imagine the fuss if that was even suggested today? Football then wasn't the dominant force it is nowadays and we just had to put up with it. The lush, green turf you dreamt of a kid was gone on and my shoes were caked in mud after the first couple of steps.

I tried to absorb the atmosphere of the half-empty stadium before making my way back towards the tunnel. As I approached, the rest of the team were walking out. The lads looked at me, wondering where I'd been, when I went into the dressing room to rejoin them. Malcolm was there and he asked if I was all right. I nodded and he said 'I just wanted you to do that on your own'. After five minutes of the match, I knew why. A cross came in, our centre half George Heslop stood on my toes and Jeff Astle rose to head the ball home for the opening goal. Trailing to one of the best cup sides of that era, we had the proverbial mountain to climb, but at least we had the players to deal with the situation. Tony Book, as ever, was the first to try and build my confidence up and he helped me through the game until we found our feet and eventually pulled off a hard-fought win in extra time thanks to goals from Mike Doyle and

Glyn Pardoe. In sending me out onto that pitch before kick-off Malcolm was trying to help me overcome the awe that Wembley induces in players. It meant I was able to handle setbacks and remain on an even keel, and that was exactly the way it panned out. It was another example of him thinking outside the box, a box that most other coaches could not escape from. He understood people and he understood football.

The big games were coming thick and fast and we finished off Academica de Coimbra at Maine Road with an extra-time winner from Tony Towers to progress to the semi-final of the Cup Winners Cup. In fact, it might have been the perfect season for me had we not faced West Ham just three days later. After that fixture, my position at the club was once again under intense scrutiny as I became a victim of one of the most talked-about goals ever screened on *Match of the Day*.

Jimmy Greaves was making his debut that day for the Hammers and everyone was aware of his record of scoring in his first match for every new club he'd played for, a record he kept intact that day. But his scoring debut for the Hammers was completely overshadowed by a goal from one of his colleagues. After the break, Mike Doyle passed the ball back to me and, as I prepared to release it, I weighed up the options. I was in half a mind to look for Bookie but I remembered he had told me at half-time that he needed time to push up after opposition attacks and that I should aim it towards the strikers instead. So I launched a kick towards the Hammers half that I thought was more than adequate and returned to the goals with my back to the play. Then, as if in a dream, the ball flew over my head, bounced in front of me and ended up in the empty net. I thought, 'Eh? Where's that come from?' just as the City fans behind the goals started shouting abuse at me and calling me a clown, among other names. It took a few seconds for me to realise that a West Ham player – it turned out to be Ronnie Boyce – had volleyed the ball back on the full from my kick to make it 4–1 in their favour. Astonishingly, he was forty-five yards out, and on the right-hand side of the pitch, so it was little wonder that I thought there was no danger. I turned around to face the other twenty-one players and the first thing I saw was Tommy Booth, one of my best mates, with one of the biggest grins I'd ever seen and shaking his head. I've never forgotten that look and it somehow took the horror of the moment away. I was still completely gutted, but right then I needed to see a friendly face and I was fortunate to see Tommy's. In his own inimitable way he was taking the piss without saying a word.

That incident has been replayed over and over ever since and it was typical of my luck that the cameras happened to be there to record it. After the game, Len Davies, one of the commissionaires who worked at Maine Road, and a dear friend of mine, came down to the dressing room and asked for me. When I came out he told me that, when I was ready, Bert Trautmann was waiting upstairs. The millstone I'd be carrying around my neck of Bert and Frank Swift's reputation suddenly felt a lot heavier. I thought, 'Shit! Did that really have to happen while Bert was watching?' I wondered what he would have to say as I got changed. Len got Bert out of the boardroom, where he'd been having a drink with the chairman and directors. We went into a side room where a lot of the players had their first drink after a game. Bert asked me how I was feeling and I told him I was devastated. He said, 'Listen, son, I'll tell you something. People have forgotten that during one of my first games for City I went up for a cross, the ball hit my shoulder and flew into the net with about thirty-five seconds on the clock. I'm telling you now to forget about today.'

Of course, the difference was that my gaffe had been on national television, which made my situation a little trickier, but to be told by one of the greatest keepers of all time that he'd been no different, that people had forgotten about his mistakes with the passage of time, really meant a lot to me. I came away thinking that because I couldn't do anything about it, there was no point dwelling on it. It made a difference and I really appreciated the fact that he sought me out to say that. Of course, nobody ever credits Ronnie Boyce with scoring a fantastic goal, but that's the life of a keeper. Bert's chat also made me realise how important it was to talk with other keepers and how valuable that kind of coaching might be to others in the future. Another seed was planted by Bert and it would grow in the fullness of time into a new career.

With a Cup Winners Cup semi-final against Schalke 04 coming up, Peter Gardner of the *Manchester Evening News* started a campaign to recall Harry Dowd, who had been out in the cold for most of the season. Gardner was then a young journalist and he obviously thought Harry, a good friend, was a better option for such a huge game. He wasn't helping my cause and there were also rumblings of discontent among the City fans but Joe and Malcolm stuck to their guns and kept me as number one for the first leg in Germany.

Before we flew out from Manchester for that game, there was an incident with my mate, Arthur Mann. Arthur and his wife, Sandra, picked me up to take me to the airport in their Morris Minor Clubman. I got in the front and Val was in the back with Arthur. I glanced at Sandra and she shook her head, so I knew something wasn't quite right. I asked Arthur if he was okay and he said he was fine, but I noticed that Sandra shook her head again after he'd said it. Just before we arrived at the airport, Arthur pulled out a bottle of pills from his jacket. He shook two into his hand and then reached into the back of the car for a half bottle of whisky, which he used to wash the tablets down.

I asked Sandra what the matter was and she said, 'Joe, he's absolutely petrified of flying.' I told Arthur he couldn't mix the pills with whisky, but he'd already polished off half the bottle. As we pulled up at the departure lounge, he got out of the car and finished the rest of the bottle. His nerves were shot, but there was no stopping him. He obviously wanted to be higher than the plane for this journey, so bad was his fear of flying. We met up with the lads and a few of them asked Arthur why he was white as a ghost and I explained what the problem was. I then went off to the toilet and while I was away, somebody went to the bar and came back with a double shot of brandy to calm him down. Talk about adding fuel to the fire. It was a time when alcohol was often used to calm the nerves and we had a bottle of whisky and brandy for each game, so all the lads, myself included, could take a quick nip to warm the cockles before we ran out. Having said that, our doctors invariably drank the lion's share.

The flight was called and I saw Arthur at the bar with an empty tumbler in front of him and one or two of the lads around him. I asked what was happening and one of the lads said that they'd bought him a double to give him Dutch courage. 'You can't do that,' I yelled. 'He's on bloody tranquilisers and he's already had half a bottle.' It was too late, though, and I had to support him all the way to the plane because he was completely wrecked by this time. We boarded the plane and I asked a stewardess if there were any seats at the back where Arthur could have a bit of peace and quiet and she said that there were. Just before we were due to take off I heard this almighty racket coming from the back of the aircraft.

Everyone turned around to see what it was and unfortunately it was Arthur, violently banging his head against the fuselage. The valium and the alcohol had begun to react and he was in a terrible state, so much so that an ambulance was called to take him for treatment. Johnny Hart and Dave Ewing had run to calm him down and moments later the medics came on board to take Arthur off.

We watched through the windows as Arthur lay on a stretcher, just to the side of the plane. Then as one of the ambulance men leaned over to see if he was okay, Arthur rose up slightly and butted him. The medic slumped next to him on the stretcher. It was like a scene from *Monty Python*, totally surreal. It was a complete one-off as far as Arthur was concerned because he was neither a drinker nor a violent man. I loved him to bits and he was as a gentle as a lamb, but his fear is not that uncommon and he wasn't the first to react so badly and he won't be the last.

I didn't play too badly in that first leg against Schalke, and I finally got to wear an all-black kit in honour of my all-time hero Lev Yashin ('The Cat'), the Russian legend who used to play for Dynamo Moscow. It was something I couldn't do in domestic matches due to strict rules and a clash with the referee's attire. We knew we had the measure of the Germans, but I prepared for the return leg by breaking my nose during a session of head tennis on the morning of the game.

Malcolm loved to play head tennis in the gym and it was something we all enjoyed and competed keenly at. There was a pillar in the middle of the gym and a rope hanging across the middle. My team was usually made up of Tommy Booth, physio Roy Bailey and me – the younger kids against Mike Doyle, Ken Mulhearn and Harry Dowd. I went up to head the ball against the wall, somebody challenged me and I ended up heading the back of his head, smashing my nose. After being patched up by Roy, I was given the all-clear to play. Thank God I did because we beat them 5–1 in one of the best team performances I'd ever experienced. Alan Oakes was magnificent that night as we took them apart. Shortly after the match, I was admitted to hospital for an operation on my shattered nose. It had been affecting my breathing and afterwards they gave me a sort of Norman helmet to wear for a week to aid the healing process. I missed the last two league games of the season and Dowdy replaced me for those games, but thankfully I was recalled and passed fit for the Cup Winners Cup final against Gornik Zabrze, which was to be played in the Prater stadium in Vienna.

Austria is a beautiful country when the sun is shining and I always remember how pleasant it was on the day of the final. We trained in the morning and then went for a look around the stadium afterwards. As we walked around the Prater, Malcolm, in his infinite wisdom, turned around and said: 'Don't worry lads. I've had a word with the grounds-man and he's promised to water the pitch all afternoon.' He'd given him a few Austrian schillings as a reward and must have been feeling very pleased with himself.

Within an hour, the heavens opened and the rain didn't stop until the early hours of the morning. We went back to the hotel and relaxed while our wives went to have their hair done for the game, but, unfortunately, the stadium had no roof and if the rain didn't ease off, the hairdos would be no more than a pleasant memory by the time we kicked off. I can't recall that much about the build up to the final. We were relaxed and happy throughout the day and travelled back to the ground in preparation for the final. One of the first things we noticed was how quiet it was around the stadium – I'd seen more people for reserve matches at Maine Road. Joe Mercer wasn't one for giving big pre-match speeches. He knew what we could do and that, man for man, we were a match for any team in the world.

We walked out into what felt like an empty stadium. It was surreal because this was a major European final and if it hadn't been for about seven thousand City fans, we'd have been playing in front of less than one thousand people. Still, crowd or no crowd, we had a job to do and got down to it from the word go. We were dominant in the early stages and thoroughly deserved to score first through Neil Young, following some great work from Franny Lee. But then Gornik came at us. It was like the Alamo for a while and they were a quality side with seven internationals, but Franny Lee scored the next goal to put us 2–0 up before the break. We were a fit, strong team of winners and though we conceded a goal in the second half, we held on to win 2–1. It was an incredible feat, but one that was largely overlooked in our own country due to the FA Cup final between Leeds and Chelsea being replayed and televised live that same evening. Our game was beamed across Europe, but at home there was no live coverage, which is a disgrace. The games should have been played on different evenings, but that's the way things panned out and whether or not we got the credit we deserved, we still won a major European trophy.

Afterwards, we had a reception in Vienna and shared a meal with the Gornik players and UEFA officials. It was a men-only occasion and our wives – who had arrived at the stadium looking like a million dollars but ended up looking like drowned rats after sitting through a torrential downpour – had to make do with a separate room. We all got back together at the hotel and had a proper celebration and I woke up with a banging headache, as we all did I hasten to add. I reckon the hotel ran dry of champagne but it's a night I'll never forget.

As we flew home to Manchester, I reflected on a momentous year. I'd been through just about every emotion it's possible to experience during my first season as a first-team regular. It had been gut-wrenching, exhilarating, disappointing and magnificent; a bizarre concoction, a rollercoaster ride. Typical City, some might say: marriage, a League Cup winner's medal, a European Cup Winners Cup winner's medal, an England under-twenty-three cap, being installed as number one and then dropped. If Manchester City were a theme-park ride, they'd be the Big One at Blackpool pleasure beach. There is no club that compares to City when it comes to pure, unbridled drama and I loved being part of it.

6

Blowing Hot and Cold

Harry Dowd and Ken Mulhearn had played their last games for City's first team and as the 1970/71 season kicked off, it was youngster Ronnie Healey who was my main challenger. Despite the disappointment of being replaced by a rookie, neither Harry nor Ken were ever anything but first class with me. I learned a lot from both men, not only as a player but also about how to behave graciously when things weren't going my way.

Before we began our summer break following our success in Vienna, we had a month-long tour of Australia to undertake. Just before boarding the plane at Manchester, Mike Summerbee came up and handed me an envelope.

'What's this for?'

'Don't say anything. Just put it in your jacket pocket.'

Of course, when I got the chance, I opened it and found about £300 inside. I spoke with some of the other lads, who said I should send it home by registered post rather than take all that money to Oz because it was a substantial amount in the early Seventies. It transpired that the money had been given to the team by a London bookie as a 'reward' for beating Sheffield Wednesday on the last day of the season. I didn't play in that game and we'd won 2–1, sending Wednesday down to the second division. Crystal Palace stayed up as a result but I wondered what it was all about; eventually, I found out. The story I was told was that it was a 'thank you' from a delighted bookmaker, who had made a packet on

Palace surviving. The bookmaker should have saved his money. The lads of that era always gave 100 per cent, no matter who they were playing. There was also the small matter of the European Cup Winners Cup final; we wanted to stay sharp for that match and that was an added incentive for us to play at the top of our game right to the end of the domestic season.

Just before we took off for Oz, club secretary Walter Griffiths gathered us together and said, 'Look lads, you've had another wonderful season and we just want you to know that, from here on in, the drinks are on the club.' We stopped short of a round of applause, but this was honey to the bees. I believe the tour Down Under was financed by sponsors, but by the time we'd finished, I understand we actually owed the tour organisers money! As you can imagine, we didn't shy away when ordering from the bar on that tour; we didn't at the best of times, and there was most definitely a drinking culture at City and at every other club from what I could tell. It certainly didn't help my waistline and that meant I wasn't at my best.

We stopped at Dusseldorf and Damascus and went on to Bahrain, Delhi and from there to Singapore. Throughout the flight, which was almost entirely in darkness, you could see this tiny, orange light intermittently moving up and down at the back of the plane. It didn't take long to suss out that it was Neil Young's cigarette! I don't think there was a time I saw him without a fag during the entire flight but it seems incredible, knowing the dangers of a fire on board an aircraft, that passengers were permitted to smoke. I'm not sure what Youngy would have done if he hadn't been able to light up; he'd probably have gone to Oz by boat.

It was a fantastic trip with no expense spared and we stayed in the best hotels, ate the best food and drank whatever we wanted. I roomed with Ian Bowyer and, on the journey from Manchester, we had an overnight stop in Singapore, arriving in mid-afternoon with a chance of a bit of sightseeing before we continued on our way. Both Ian and I freshened up at the hotel before going downstairs to meet up with the rest of the lads. Unfortunately, they were nowhere to be seen and, after checking at the front desk, we realised they had already gone out. We asked the staff at reception where the boys might have gone and they told us they'd all headed for 'Boogie Street', wherever that was. It gets worse.

We caught a cab to Boogie Street and were dropped off at the top of a road filled with flashing neon signs, bars and god-knows-what-else for as far as the eye could see. I'd never experienced anything like it and it wasn't hard to see how the area had got its name. There was me and Ian – two naive kids from working-class backgrounds – slap bang in the middle of Babylon. We'd barely left the cab when two gorgeous girls approached us. It suddenly dawned us what they were, and we turned tail and ran like two frightened rabbits; let's just say they would have expected us to have paid for the privilege of their company. The lads had gone to a nightclub, but we ended up in the relative safety of the hotel, had a few pints and turned in. We spent the rest of the following day lounging around the hotel pool and soaking up the sun. Neither of us used lotion like the rest of the squad and later on we both felt ill, the victims of sunstroke. It was turning out to be a bit of a nightmare and we hadn't even reached our ultimate destination. We flew on to Perth, both feeling rotten and very sorry for ourselves. We must have looked a right pair of numpties, red raw and hardly able to move, but sometimes you have to learn the hard way. Ask the other lads about the flight to Australia and they'll likely regale you with exotic stories of beautiful women, drink and sunshine. Ask Ian and me and you'd think we'd been on a different tour.

Harry Dowd and I shared keeping duties in Oz and the games were well attended with a lot of ex-pat City fans, especially in Brisbane where there was a large crowd. The Aussies tend to make a match a family day out with barbecues and plenty of pre-match entertainment and I enjoyed the atmosphere. I thought it would be a great place to live and work.

In my opinion we got some bad press during the tour, particularly from Eamonn Dunphy who would later ghost Roy Keane's autobiography but was then a rookie journalist. I thought that Dunphy – who hadn't had much of a playing career himself – was particularly harsh in one article: my interpretation of it was that we were nothing but drunks in search of a jolly. There was no denying we enjoyed ourselves, but it never got out of hand and we never harmed or upset anybody. We were professionals once we stepped over the line to play; we were never disrespectful to our hosts and gave our usual polished performances. Apart from anything else Joe and Malcolm would never have tolerated anything less than total professionalism. Besides, we won six out of the seven games comfortably, drawing the other, and if the lads did let their hair down, so what? We'd had a long, exhausting season and won two trophies. In my view Dunphy's articles had blackened the good name of Manchester City. Eventually, we took him to task for it.

During a meal in Sydney, which Dunphy attended, Mike Doyle became more and more agitated by the Irishman's behaviour. The player-turned-journalist was, to my mind, obnoxious and outspoken throughout the meal and, when the pair went for a pee at the same time, it didn't take a genius to work out that Doyley would set the record straight in the privacy of the rest rooms. A few of the lads sussed this out and just managed to stop Mike from knocking ten bells out of Dunphy, who by now looked as though he was wishing he'd taken up another profession. It was a disappointing end to a great tour but we turned on the style in our final game against New South Wales – winning 4–0 – just to prove a point. Why Dunphy penned that series of articles I'll never know. I disagreed totally with almost every word he wrote and I am sure our performances in Oz were testament to our professionalism. Only he knows the answers, but I think that was one of his first jobs and I'm sure he learned a lot from the experience and he obviously went on to be very successful as a journalist, broadcaster and author. The pen may well be mightier than the sword, but his pen was no match for a Mike Doyle right hook.

We returned home and rested up for the remainder of the summer, before returning with our batteries recharged for the 1970/71 campaign. Unfortunately, however, it turned out to be a case of 'after the Lord Mayor's show'. We started really well, winning six and drawing two of our opening eight games, putting us top of the table for several weeks, but although we only lost three of our first seventeen league games, the season imploded after Christmas.

We were left with defending our European Cup Winners Cup title having crashed out of the League Cup at the first hurdle to Carlisle, a team we'd been expected to beat comfortably. We'd got used to receiving winners medals and there were no teams that scared us in the competition. However, we almost shot ourselves in the foot after being paired with Linfield in the first round of the Cup Winners Cup. We just edged the first leg against the Irish part-timers at Maine Road, with Colin Bell scoring the only goal of the game, but the return match in Belfast was unforgettable for a number of reasons – none of them good. Linfield are the Rangers of Belfast and so we were on our way to a Loyalist hotbed at the height of the Troubles in Northern Ireland. To make matters worse there had been sectarian violence on the streets and several high-profile incidents between the British Army and the IRA in the days leading up to the match. Let's just say there was a very intimidating atmosphere inside Windsor Park, which was, incidentally, packed to the rafters. The Northern Irish people love their football and they were vociferous in their support, willing their favourites to take the biggest scalp in the club's history. With only one goal to pull back, the excitement boiled over and things started to get nasty. Behind my goal, bottles and other missiles began raining down from the terraces and the people throwing them made no secret of their intended target: me. It was unnerving to say the least and Linfield manager Billy Bingham had to come out and plead with his fans not to force the game to be abandoned. He asked for calm, and eventually we were able to resume. Linfield played out of their skins, winning 2–1 on the night, with only a Franny Lee penalty ensuring we squeezed through on away goals. We'd been outplayed and could have had no complaints if we'd gone out. The crowd trouble took the focus away from a fantastic performance by Linfield and I don't believe they got the credit they deserved for that victory.

I heard a teenager had been shot by security forces after running through a roadblock while we were there and that seemed to have heightened the tensions. We were relieved to get on the plane and fly home straight after the match. In fact, we had an armoured car escort us to the airport and I believe there were SAS officers on our coach. As we drove through the more populated areas on the way to Belfast airport, I realised how tall I was as I looked around the coach, head and shoulders above everyone else, before realising the rest of the lads were crouching down in their seats! It was sad, given that my mother's side of the family originate from Belfast and they are all warm and generous people, as are the majority of folk from the Province.

We also faced Bologna in the pointless Anglo-Italian Cup that month, one of nine games we played during September 1970 – and modern managers whinge about having to play too much football. We played the first leg in Italy, staying at Rimini, and the lads treated it as a bit of a holiday if truth be told. We had a day on the beach before taking on the Italians and losing 1–0, but nobody held the trophy in much esteem and we went out after drawing the second leg 2–2 at Maine Road. Losing to

Linfield and Carlisle seemed to knock our confidence and what should have been another fantastic season turned out to be a damp squib. We seemed to have an Achilles heel against teams we were expected to ease past yet excelled against higher-quality outfits. Our 1–0 win against top Hungarian side Honved was a perfect example, as few teams ever left Budapest with anything other than a defeat. But then we were almost knocked out of the FA Cup by non-league Wigan in a nervy third-round tie at Maine Road and edged it 1–0.

We came face to face with Gornik Zabrze again in the third round of the Cup Winners Cup. I was the coldest I'd ever been in my life during the first leg in Poland and would happily have worn a fur coat, hat and gloves. The game would have never been allowed in England because the pitch was white – frozen solid with coloured lines – but because that type of weather was fairly common in Poland, it went ahead. Nothing went right on that trip and it began badly when we boarded the coach after landing at the airport. Fumes were leaking in from underneath and seeping into the cabin and it was surprising nobody suffered carbon-monoxide poisoning. At the hotel the lift broke down with several members of the team stuck inside. Little things like that can upset a team.

Gornik were obviously out to avenge their defeat in the final from the previous season and were far better prepared, physically and mentally, than us. Their players wore filed-down metal studs, not dissimilar to running spikes, and we just couldn't cope with them or the advantage it gave them. It must have been how Spurs felt during the Ballet on Ice back in 1968 when we worse similar footwear. The crowd was immense and intimidating with around 100,000 fans crammed in and we were well beaten by two goals to nil, though it should have been more. I wore tracksuit bottoms and padding to protect myself and I reckon I would have been suffering from hypothermia had I not been kept so busy by the likes of the brilliant Wlodzimierz Lubanski and co.

Afterwards, my elbows came up like balloons and it was yet another hostile atmosphere we couldn't escape from quickly enough. They'd given their best yet we still were in with a shout and we took great heart from that, enough, in fact, to beat them 2–0 at Maine Road and force a replay on neutral ground, which turned out to be Copenhagen of all places, although I didn't play. With the extra travel and expense for both teams, it's no wonder penalty shoot-outs were eventually brought in to settle ties. We won 3–1 in the deciding match and were now just one round away from appearing in our second successive final.

Meanwhile, Val was expecting our first child, and, at the beginning of April, our daughter Sara was born. To be honest, I didn't have a clue what to do or what was expected of me during the labour and I ended up waiting around, aptly, in the waiting room. When a nurse came in and informed me Val was close to giving birth, I told her that the other two blokes who were also in there were ahead of me in the 'queue'! It sounded ridiculous as I said it – when did babies ever arrive on a first-come, first-served basis? As my little girl was being delivered, one of the doctors turned to me and said, 'Don't you faint for God's sake. There's nobody in this hospital who will be able to pick you up.'

It was an amazing, humbling moment as Sara came into the world and it suddenly made me realise how financially fragile my situation was. As things stood, if I had a bad season I could be on the scrapheap and I had a young family to take care of. I now had much more onerous responsibilities and I knew that I had to work harder than ever to provide for my family. The glory of my first full season in football was just yesterday's fish-and-chip paper and the birth of my first child brought me back down to earth with a bump. It was all about how I handled things and I was more determined than ever to be a success. Your life changes forever when you become a parent and the whole fabric of our daily lives was turned upside down; everything from eating habits to sleeping patterns now revolved around Sara. Nevertheless I still needed to train and play football, so there was a period of adapting as a family. Of course Val was fantastic and ensured that I could concentrate on my job.

We were living in Sale Moor in our first house, a three-bedroom semi that set us back the princely sum of £3,500. Living within walking distance of most of my family helped Val a lot, because she'd completely changed her life and left her family and friends behind in Shrewsbury. It was also a great leveller for me not to be isolated from the real world. I could pop down to the pub for the odd pint; nobody would bother me and I could also walk around the neighbourhood without any problems because most people there had known me for years. I was plain old Joe, a local lad who just happened to play for one of the biggest clubs in the country.

When we had a babysitter, Val and I would occasionally go into

Manchester for a night out and, when we did, invariably it would be with the Manns. There is one evening that sticks in my memory. Val and I had gone to Annabel's in town with Arthur and Sandra. It was a favourite spot for a lot of the City and United lads and George Best was there, as he was much of the time. He came over and bought us all a drink, had a chat and was as charming as ever. We left about eleven and George seemed sober, relaxed and in good spirits. A couple of days later there was a story in the press that he'd punched a girl in the face later that same night. The story I heard was that he was alone in a corner when a girl started pestering him. He tried to get her to leave him alone and there was some contact with the girl as he pushed her away. Inevitably, it was blown out of all proportion; at least, that's what I was told by people who'd been there.

I felt sorry for George because he was such a lovely, generous guy but an easy target for any number of vultures, gold-diggers and hangers-on. I'd occasionally call in at his fashion boutique in the city centre and he'd always open a bottle of champagne and pour me a glass of bubbly; George was never less than charming company. Yet he was a very lonely man, and, because nobody ever told him to act any differently, it was inevitable that the bottle would eventually get hold of him and he never really managed to shake free.

Later, when his drinking worsened, I took part in a charity game between Liverpool and an all-Ireland side in Dublin. George was supposed to kick the game off but he couldn't even stand up. A few years later, he was scheduled to speak at an after-dinner event at Tytherington golf club, but, when I went to see where he was, I found him and realised he was too drunk to say anything. He was a gentleman and a decent human being, blessed with extraordinary skill.

As for me, things began to look up at club level. I was recalled to the first team when passed fit and took my place in goal against Huddersfield Town at Maine Road. It was good timing on my part with the Cup Winners Cup semi-final against, of all clubs, Chelsea, just four days away. The team was in the middle of a dreadful run of form. We'd failed to score in eight of the previous twelve games, five of them 0–0 draws, so it wasn't the best way to prepare for such an important game. Injuries to Mike Summerbee, Neil Young, Colin Bell, Glyn Pardoe, Franny Lee, Alan Oakes, Tony Book, Tommy Booth, Mike Doyle, Tony

Towers and of course me had decimated the team at various points in the season and we went into the first leg against Chelsea at Stamford Bridge missing six first-team regulars.

In many ways it was a glimpse of the future as the all-conquering City team built by Mercer and Allison slowly began to fall apart. Players were getting older, the magic was fading and three successive mid-table finishes led many to believe that we were no more than a decent cup side. Still, better that than nothing at all and we went into the semi-final knowing it was a tall order with so many absentees and on the back of yet another blank weekend following a 1–0 defeat at Huddersfield. Against Chelsea, despite a very young City side fighting valiantly, we lost 1–0. We'd been without some of our best players but had still done enough to have a chance of turning the tie around at Maine Road, even if it meant fielding a team of walking wounded.

Sadly, for me, I managed just two more league games before cutting my knee in training and getting a nasty infection that blew it up like a balloon. There was real concern that the osteomyelitis had returned and I was rushed to hospital for an operation before it got any worse. It turned out it was simply an infected cut and no more; I had to have the bursa inside my knee cap removed because that was the source of the infection. My season was over and despite an injured Buzzer making a gallant effort in the return with Chelsea, we lost 1–0 again and finished the season empty handed for the first time in four years. We'd ended the season by winning just one of our last eighteen games; relegation form, however you looked at it.

I spent the summer of 1971 recuperating from my knee op in readiness for the 1971/72 season when the old boys would have one last hurrah . . . and things really began to kick-off.

7

A Reckless Throw of the Dice

Wyn Davies had arrived from Newcastle United during the summer and he added a new dimension to our attack for the start of the 1971/72 season. After the way the previous campaign had flat-lined after Christmas, I'm not sure what the City fans were expecting us to do – probably win a trophy or get relegated. Scoring goals had been a big problem and the lack of them was the main reason we'd struggled in recent seasons. With Ian Mellor and Buzzer playing on the wings, we needed a big target man in the middle, and, at that time, Wyn was one of the best in the country. He proved a tremendous asset to our side. I enjoyed playing in the same side as Wyn and training with him; he was a terrific man to know and it helped me to have to deal with such an awkward player every day at Platt Lane. He could hold the ball up, he was as brave as a lion and he gave me a target to aim for when I launched the ball up-field, something that had been sorely missing.

I felt we had a settled team again and youngsters like Willie Donachie, Ian Mellor and Tony Towers brought plenty to the table as they replaced the likes of Glyn Pardoe, Neil Young and Tony Coleman – big boots to fill, but the kids were doing well. One of my best mates, Ian Bowyer, had given up trying to win over the City fans and joined Leyton Orient; he would prove his critics wrong in later years as he became an integral part of Brian Clough's hugely successful Nottingham Forest side of the mid-to-late Seventies. I couldn't have been happier for him. I often wonder what might have happened had things worked out for him at Maine Road, but his face didn't fit with certain people. It happens in football.

This would be the year when I began to do something that would become a habit and it was born mainly out of superstition. I'm not sure exactly which game it was that I decided not to watch our penalties being taken, but it was something that stayed with me throughout my career. I recall seeing Franny miss from the spot in one game and feeling that somehow I'd influenced it by watching him so I decided to crouch down and face the other way every time we got a penalty. The crowd reaction would tell me all I needed to know.

The 71/72 campaign would be a record-breaking one for Franny, who would score an incredible fourteen spot kicks as we started to get our act together. Of course, I saw enough of his penalty expertise in training, where he regularly beat me from the spot. He would smash the ball as hard as he could and invariably score; you couldn't work out what he had planned and even if you guessed right it was like trying to catch a cannonball. Franny had such belief in his ability and emanated an amazing aura of confidence; I regard him as one of the best players this country has ever produced. You get a unique perspective being a goalkeeper and I count myself lucky to have seen some fantastic footballers over the years. Franny was one of the quickest forwards over five or six yards, and, as a striker, that's all you need; the ability to get to a loose ball first and put the opportunity away.

We would have won the league in 1971/72 but for one decision. It was a decision that changed the whole course of history for the club – the signing of Rodney Marsh from Queen's Park Rangers for £200,000. We were going very strongly and were at the top of the table with just five defeats in thirty-three games. Liverpool, Leeds United and Derby were also going full pelt for the title, but we had the edge and there was something extra in our team that looked set to carry us over the finishing line ahead of the pack. Tony Towers was one of the unsung heroes of a well-oiled machine that was ticking over like a Rolls going into March. Everyone knew their jobs and everything had slotted into place at the right time; there were no passengers. The line-up had hardly changed since October so to bring in a new player for the last lap was utter madness, especially such a maverick talent as Rodney. I thought he was a fantastic player with wonderful individual skill, but therein lay the problem; he had individual ability but in my view he wasn't enough of a team player.

It wasn't his fault. The decision to bring him in was down to Malcolm, who'd convinced Joe that he was the man to ensure we won the league. Malcolm felt we needed more flair in the side; he perhaps saw us as too functional, as grafters. The plain truth was that the team didn't need Rodney Marsh at that time; we were doing very nicely without him. It was all about timing and had Marsh arrived in the summer of 1972 he would have given us options and most likely he would have been joining the newly crowned league champions. There was also a discernible effect on morale: some players suspected he was being paid more than anyone else, and this, when allied to doubts about his work rate, was undoubtedly a problem for some players. It was a reckless throw of the dice when there was no need to gamble, but that's what Malcolm was all about.

A crowd of 53,322 crammed into Maine Road for Marsh's first game in March 1972, a 1–0 win over Chelsea. Perhaps things wouldn't be so bad after all. But Rodney wasn't match fit, having been out of the QPR side with a groin strain prior to his arrival, though you could see the potential on his debut, half fit or not. At this crucial stage of the season, however, we started dropping points against sides we had been beating easily a few weeks earlier and we lost the initiative. I was to play no part in the run-in after injuring my back against Chelsea and missed the next seven games. We won just two of those and the league was lost. What had potentially been a title-deciding last match of the season against Derby, now champions, was no more than academic and our 2–0 win had a hollow feel.

It is well documented that Marsh's style disrupted the free-flowing football we had been playing all season and there's not much more to say that hasn't already been said. His arrival proved one thing beyond all doubt: Malcolm's power had reached previously unseen levels and his thirst to be his own man was slowly edging Joe Mercer out of the door. We'd finished fourth in the table despite one last great effort from our big-name players and it was going to be difficult to pick ourselves up for the 1972/73 season having felt we'd lost the title rather than Derby winning it.

The fall-out from that failure changed the club forever and the family values City had always adhered to were ruthlessly cast aside. I found out Joe Mercer was no longer our manager when I came in for pre-season training prior to the 1972/73 season and it was a complete shock. I heard that Joe had been asked to 'move upstairs' but he had no intention of doing that and I know his wife Nora, a wonderful woman, was devastated about the way things were handled. I'm not sure exactly what happened but to lose a man of his experience and charisma could only be bad for the club. Joe moved on to Coventry and Malcolm had his big chance to manage City on his own, a role I believe he had coveted for some time. I think he wanted people to recognise his contribution and if he was calling the shots and we were winning trophies, he'd get it.

It was a partnership that should never have been broken up. Mercer and Allison complemented each other perfectly. Joe was respected by everyone in football; he had a great track record at the highest level as both player and manager. A thoughtful, shrewd character he was very much the father figure at Maine Road, and his vast experience in the game enabled him to make reasoned judgements about players and tactics. Malcolm, by contrast, was like your big brother. He was very close to the players – too close many felt – and would often socialise with us. He wanted to be our best pal, which would inevitably lead to difficulties when he had to discipline someone. I feel that it is important for management to have a good working relationship with players but to keep them at arm's length; otherwise it becomes more difficult to take the hard decisions that are so often required in football. Nevertheless Malcolm was a great coach, and was especially effective when he had the time and space to get on with that part of the job. With Joe as senior partner Malcolm was able to innovate and he did that with considerable success. The list is almost endless: fitness monitoring with the University of Salford; special conditioning to build-up muscles; running days with athletes like Derek Ibbotson and Joe Lancaster; advice on diet; specialist coaching for goalkeepers. These programmes may be commonplace now but they were revolutionary at the time.

Now that he was in overall charge Malcolm's style didn't change that much and he still did the things he'd done when he was just the coach, but I felt he missed the steadying hand of Joe Mercer. A lot of people, including me, owe Malcolm such a lot and the press loved him because he was never short of a good quote. The fact is, however, that you need different attributes to manage, especially at that level. Put simply, he didn't have what it takes.

I was still struggling with a back injury, but felt fit enough to start the new season. My relationship with the City fans still blew hot and cold; there was no strong bond between us and things would come to a head over the next couple of years. I recall being at an evening event with Val, which Nobby Stiles also attended. There was this guy having a go at me, winding me up, singing stupid songs and making sly comments. Eventually, I walked over, picked him up by his collar and gave serious consideration to knocking him through the wall. But I'd learned from my experience in Bilbao, and, through gritted teeth, let him go. I had to watch my step and I kept my self-control, even though my blood was boiling.

We started the 72/73 campaign badly, losing five of the first six league games and despite winning three of the next five, we were heavily beaten at Birmingham (4–1) and Stoke City (5–1) in the next few trips on the road. It's funny – and as a keeper you might think, 'well, you would say that' – but just because five goals have gone past you doesn't necessarily mean you've had a bad game. People will see the score and assume that the goalie has had a shocker, but sometimes he might have prevented a much heavier defeat. It's a strange position and no wonder people say you have to be mad to play there.

That said, I was a worrier and I was always wondering about the future and what was in store for me. I recall Malcolm sitting in the changing room after a training session and saying: 'This kid is going to be one the best keepers in the world,' in reference to me. Reserve goalie Ronnie Healey turned around and asked, 'Well what does that make me?' Malcolm winked at Ronnie and replied, 'One of the best substitutes in the country.' I'd gone from a father–son relationship with Joe Mercer to a big-brother–younger-brother relationship with Malcolm. He'd sit at the bar and buy drinks for you and be the life and soul of the party, but he needed to distance himself from us because there would be times when he had to make difficult decisions or leave people out. He was just too close to the players and I think it affected his judgement and condemned his time as manager to failure. He was heavily influenced by the likes of Buzzer and Franny and fiercely loyal to people like Tony Book, whom he'd rescued from non-league football. But a manager has to be completely autonomous when it comes to making decisions, even if it means disappointing those he has a close relationship with.

Peter Swales had now arrived as club chairman and things were changing constantly. Swales enjoyed a close working relationship with Malcolm and influenced his thinking, which had never been the style of the previous chairman, Albert Alexander, a lovely old bloke who liked things to run along smoothly without unnecessary chopping and changing. I think Swales was probably the first of a new breed of chairmen: wealthy, hands on and involved in all aspects of the club from the boardroom to the pitch. He was a sharp businessman with a ruthless streak, but he loved Manchester City, nobody ever doubted that.

Rodney Marsh had by this time settled in and contrary to popular belief, I never had a problem with him either personally or as a team-mate. Sure he was a bit of a Flash Harry and he came into a team made up of Northern lads from working-class backgrounds so it's fair to say he didn't really fit, but I'm not sure Rodney's ambition in life was ever to fit in. In later years comments I made about him were taken out of context and if this is a chance to put the record straight, I'll take it. He had his flaws and things had to be right for Rodney for him to turn on the style, but he was a talented lad with an innate ability to trip himself up and win free kicks or penalties. With Marsh and Franny Lee in the same team, I wouldn't have been surprised if defenders felt like taking the day off when they saw the team sheet. It was during the 72/73 campaign that Franny scored a 'Hand of God' goal away to Spurs, long before Diego Maradona's improvised goal against England. It wasn't the first time, either, and he disguised his hand well as he lunged towards a cross and from most angles it looked like it had been a header. That was Franny, crafty as a fox and a born winner who would do anything to make sure he was the one smiling at the end of a game.

Shortly after that rare victory during another flat season, we went down 5–1 at Wolves and it was obvious that the Allison era was in its death throes. There was the air of an empire in decline about the place and many of the stars who had made the club great were coming to the end of their careers. Joe Mercer had gone and with him went a lot of stability so when Malcolm realised things were only going to get worse I think he jumped before he was pushed, though whether the board would ever have sacked him is debatable. I wasn't surprised, but it brought an amazing era at Maine Road to a close and, love him or loathe him, the place was going to be a lot less colourful in his absence.

One of the backroom boys, Johnny Hart, took over, on 30 March 1973. I'd always got along really well with him so I had no problems on a personal level. Johnny had been one of the coaches the day I was signed by City and we went back a long way. He was a lovely guy to work with and had a vast knowledge of the game, but I must admit it was a big shock to most of us when he was promoted to manager. Deep down, I had my doubts as to whether he was the right man to take on such a huge task and, unfortunately, within six months, Johnny was forced to resign due to ill health. To watch him go downhill and age ten years within weeks of taking on the role wasn't pleasant. There were some strong characters in the dressing room and it must have been a massive ordeal for him. It was probably a huge relief when he finally gave up the ghost before any irreparable damage was done, though it would be several months before that actually happened.

My second daughter, Emma, was born on 23 March 1973 and the club's attitude to her birth is also a good illustration of the sea change that has occurred in football. Modern players believe it is almost their divine right to be present when their children are born. But Malcolm was surprised that I wanted to be with Val at the birth, insisting that I wouldn't be of much use to her. It wasn't as if I was asking for time off; I had turned up for training as normal and made a dash to the hospital after it finished. However, family matters aside, it wasn't all good news: Malcolm, in one of his last acts as manager, had dropped me for the run-in to give Ronnie Healey a chance, but perhaps after becoming a father again it looked as if I needed a rest!

8

Attacked by the Stretford End

After finishing eleventh in 1972/73, we headed out for an end-of-season trip to Greece to wind down. We were there to play Olympiakos, who were owned by one of the Goulandris brothers, a multi-millionaire shipping magnate who had made connections with City after a friendly the previous season. We stayed at a top hotel and had originally been scheduled to play just one game during a sunshine break, but were asked to play a second game to help cover our travel expenses. Unusual, but it meant more time in a beautiful country so nobody complained.

The drinking culture within the club continued unchallenged and it was on trips like this that the serious boozing took place as the players let their hair down. It was the end of a disappointing campaign and we were determined to enjoy ourselves and put it behind us via a succession of binges. Franny was the 'chairman' and so he would choose the drinks we had to down, subject to a specific task he set. My task was to drink pints of white wine in one go, as directed by chairman Lee, and, hardly surprisingly, it was on that trip that I first saw somebody turn physically green. We'd flown into Athens and had been having a few beers on the plane, and, when we boarded the coach, we started on the duty free at the back of the bus.

We got to the hotel and Buzzer did a body swerve as we got off, with his legs no longer under his control. We settled in our rooms and it wasn't long before we had an invite from 'Mr Chairman' asking us round to his apartment for drinks. I trundled along and Buzzer was there, sitting next to Franny – they were great mates – on the veranda facing the sea. Franny was puffing away on a huge cigar and he inhaled a mouthful of smoke and blew it into Buzzer's face. I watched Mike's face turn green and moments later he was violently sick everywhere. Afterwards, I went back to my room and as I dozed on the bed there was a knock on the door. I was sharing the apartment with Marshy and I opened the door, but couldn't see anyone. I thought it was odd so went back to have another look and there on the floor was Rodney, out like a light and absolutely paralytic. I dragged him into the room by his heels so he could sleep it off. There were one or two hangovers the next morning, but it was a fantastic trip and I've a lot of great memories from our time in Greece. I didn't realise it at the time but I could have carried on in the same vein for years to come had a transfer offer been accepted by City.

We travelled out to see Goulandris, who lived in an area called Piraeus. His house was carved out of the side of a mountain, around three hundred feet above sea level. It was an amazing home and because his wife didn't want to be overlooked, he bought the whole mountain – no big deal to a man with his wealth. The whole property, surrounded by armed guards, was pure indulgence and beautifully designed with a football pitch built to one side of the house. Goulandris was football mad and could have been the Roman Abramovich of his day had he so wished. He was a great character and seemed delighted that the Manchester City squad were paying him a personal visit. We ate and drank whatever we wanted, lounged around in the pool and even had an impromptu knock about, resulting in a smashed window. It looked like it was worth a few bob and there were one or two concerned looks from our lads, but we were told not to worry about it and within seconds there were servants clearing up the mess. Not long after that a new window unit, with exactly the same design, was in place as though nothing had happened.

We played Olympiakos and lost 2–1 and a week later we drew 0–0 against them and it was after that game I was told the real reason we'd played the second game was so the Greek side could take another look and then buy me. It was news to me and I only heard about it when one of the tour organisers told me in confidence. I was flattered by their interest but I would never have gone to play football in Greece; it just wasn't for me. We returned to Manchester and I was happy to get back to my wife and daughters and normality.

Later that summer, our pre-season tour of Scotland provided further proof that Johnny Hart's days as manager were numbered. Sometimes it's the smallest things that say such a lot. We had travelled north of the border to play friendlies against Aberdeen and St Johnstone, and normally that would mean training, a bit of relaxation and playing matches. I was surprised, then, to see Buzzer and Franny pack a car up with fishing gear and disappear for several hours while we were there. I'd never known anything like that before because it wasn't a holiday and the lads were meant to stick together in preparation for the new season.

Johnny was clearly finding it difficult to deal with the stronger characters in the squad, especially after effectively being their buddy for so many years. He did engineer something of a coup, however, by signing another of my boyhood heroes, Denis Law, from United. Tommy Docherty had decided to let him leave on a free transfer and Johnny was the first in a long line of managers who wanted to sign Denis. When he walked into our dressing room for the first time as a City player, I reminded him of the time he'd raked my hand in my first Manchester derby and he just put his hands up and said, 'Steady big man, steady!' He was a great character and still a terrific player, even though this was his swansong. In fact, his gentle persona off the pitch was nothing like the man who wore the number-nine shirt on a Saturday afternoon, who was anything but a gentleman, but perhaps it was that side to his game that had helped him get to the top and stay there for so long.

He scored twice on his debut against Birmingham City but he always came across to me as a United player, which I suppose given his history with them is understandable. He was a phenomenal man and it was a pleasure to play alongside him for a year. I roomed with Denis that season and he was always the lord and master. He was always drinking tea – he was fanatical about it – and I was designated as the brew boy. Rooming with Denis was guaranteed to keep your feet on the ground, that's for sure. He was a lovely man to be around, but his goal against United in the last game of season 1973/74 proved that he was one of the game's most instinctive goal-scorers – he knew what a goal against the club he loved would mean, but he was leading City's line now and his job was to score goals, whatever the consequences.

On a personal level, however, things were about to come to a head for me at City and the fall-out would leave me considering not just my future at Maine Road, but also in football. We'd made a decent start to the season and had taken ten points from a possible sixteen when we travelled to newly promoted Burnley for what was expected to be a blood-and-thunder Lancashire derby. For the whole team it turned out to be a particularly bad day at the office but, being the last line of defence, the blame fell squarely on my shoulders. I freely acknowledge it was a day to forget all round, but certain things happened that left a bad taste in my mouth for years to come. We were under the cosh when Mike Doyle controlled a cross and played the ball back to me. But the pass didn't have enough pace and, as the Burnley striker slid in, the ball went under my body and trickled towards the line. I tried to scramble back, sliding in at top speed but ended up marooned in the back of the net looking like an idiot. It was my job to keep the ball out and I didn't care what it looked like, but the fact remained it was a goal, despite my efforts. I kicked the ball up field and didn't see Mike Doyle run to the manager's dugout, where he let it be known in no uncertain terms what he thought of me as a keeper and as a man. A guy on the Burnley bench – a former goalkeeper if memory serves – jumped up in my defence and told Mike to worry about his own game but the damage had been done. We lost 3–0 and afterwards Ken Barnes told me Doyley had asked, 'What's that fat bastard doing in goals for us?' I couldn't believe he'd do that because we were meant to be a team. It left me feeling cold towards Mike for a number of years.

The local press didn't help my cause, either. They were constantly referring to my height and weight as if I was a circus freak. I was the tallest player in the league but dubbing me as a 'monster keeper' was a little over the top, in my opinion. The headlines that followed the Turf Moor game were all about City's search for a new keeper and a list of possible candidates. I'd obviously been drinking in the last-chance saloon with certain people due to one or two high-profile mistakes and now there was something close to a witch-hunt taking place. People look for scapegoats when things aren't going well – always have, always will – and I would need to ride the storm out if I was to salvage my career with the Blues.

I was dropped for the next game with Ronnie Healey replacing me, and, within two weeks, Keith MacRae was signed from Motherwell for a hefty £100,000, a world-record fee at the time for a goalkeeper. Ian St

John was his manager and he told me in later years that they couldn't believe the fee City had paid and they celebrated by painting their main stand! I knew a little bit about Keith, but had no idea the club had even been looking at anybody else. There had been speculation, but this sent a clear message out that the management didn't think I was up to the task of being City's number one. I didn't have a problem with Keith, but I knew he wasn't as good as I was, which isn't me being big-headed; what happened in later years would prove that beyond any reasonable doubt. I knew from our first training session that there was more to my game than his, but it was the management I had to convince. Keith was a nice lad and we got on well; there was no animosity between us and there were no airs or graces about him.

I was hurt by the events of that month and, in all honesty, wanted out. I didn't feel there was a future for me at the club and after considering my options, I asked for a transfer. Bobby Charlton was manager at Preston and he put in an offer to take me to Deepdale – for how much I don't know – but the club turned it down. I was still only twenty-five, but needed to be playing first-team football at that stage of my career. I had a young family to feed and being in the reserves meant my wages went down because there were no appearance fees, no win bonuses and no crowd bonuses.

I did my best and worked hard in training because that was all I could do. The club weren't desperate to offload me so I had to dig in and wait for a chance. Then, to compound my problems, I broke my jaw during a practice match at the Silver Wings training ground in Timperley. I was badly concussed, though I didn't realise it at the time and played on. Later I would have no memory of the game whatsoever. I came round a little in the changing rooms and Dave Ewing asked if I was okay and I told him my jaw was hurting. I asked him what had happened. 'What do you mean?' he asked. 'How did I end up in here?' I replied. Everything had been a blur, but apparently I took a boot in my face diving at John Gannon's feet. It had been an accident – an occupational hazard in my job – but I carried on, dazed, and running on autopilot.

It turned out I'd broken my jaw and had to have it wired up, meaning I could only eat liquidised foods through a straw for the next few weeks, but, despite the discomfort, I lost one-and-a-half stones and felt fitter and leaner than I could remember in years. Fate had worked in my favour and even though I'd had to break my jaw to start the second phase of my career, the pain was a small price to pay. During my recovery period, Johnny Hart left his post as manager of City and I was glad he did because if he'd carried on much longer, they might have had to carry him out of Maine Road in a box. A new man coming in meant I had a chance to start from scratch and looking trimmer and feeling better than I had done at any other time since my amateur days, I felt confident that I could reclaim the number-one jersey from Keith.

On 24 November 1973, Ron Saunders, manager of Norwich City, was named as the new boss and the first time I saw him was at the top of the stairs inside Maine Road. He stopped me and asked, 'What are you doing in the reserves? I've always wanted to work with you.' I said I'd been injured and was just regaining my fitness and he then told me I was one of the best goalkeepers in the country and he was looking forward to me proving it. It was just the boost I needed. I felt ten feet tall because I knew that Saunders would give me a chance. In fact, I was recalled for the New Year's Day clash with Stoke City and kept a clean sheet, but, in the interim I played against Manchester United at reserve level and got another whack on the jaw. Fortunately, I didn't break it this time but I did lose a few teeth and was out for a fortnight or so, which took the wind out of my sails. Keith resumed his place in the first team and played out of his skin in the next six games, conceding just two goals. That ensured he retained his spot for the 1974 League Cup final, and deservedly so. We lost 2–1 to Wolves and I sat in the stand watching impassively alongside Alan Oakes. On the coach home, Oakey said that he thought it was wrong that two of the most influential City players – him and me – had been watching rather than on the pitch playing. The next game, away to Leeds, I found myself back in the team again. I then played against United at Maine Road and then against Sheffield United, where my bad luck struck again as I conceded a goal straight from a corner – the only goal of the game – and I admit it was totally my fault.

I just couldn't seem to take a step forward without having to take a couple back. It was soul destroying because I was getting a reputation for shooting myself in the foot, not dissimilar to David James in his early days. The most crushing blow to my morale was still to come, when Ron Saunders came up to me afterwards and said, 'Now I understand why the directors don't want you in the team.' He'd gone from one extreme to the other in a matter of weeks and it was clear that he would bow under the pressure he was getting from upstairs. Clearly, there were people within the club who had it in for me and while I didn't help myself with errors like the one that cost us the game against Sheffield United, it hurt. Another problem was that Saunders was an odd manager to work under, full of his own beliefs and ideas. In fact, one of the strangest training sessions I'd ever taken part in was under his tenure; we were told to go on the weights for twenty minutes and, when we'd finished, that was it and we were off home again. You knew you'd worked, but it was totally different from what we'd been used to.

He once told Doyley, 'Listen, I don't want my back four to play football. If you get the ball, just lump it forward and we'll go from there.' The trouble was, we had some cultured defenders and that went against their nature. Then there was Franny and Buzzer, two wily pros who were as much part of Manchester City as the Kippax. They were up against a man with a reputation as a strict disciplinarian so the sparks were bound to fly. Saunders used to stand naked in front of the mirrors after we'd had a bath and pinch his skin and tell anyone who was listening, 'See that? Not an ounce of fat on me.' Whoever he was trying to impress, it was failing miserably. When the ground outside was hard he used to take me into the gym at Maine Road, lay mats down and conduct shooting practice. As he shot he told me to dive out of the way of the ball. I told him I had enough trouble diving in the way of the ball and thought what he was telling me to do was ridiculous. How could it possibly benefit me? He never explained what was behind his thinking; I just couldn't do it and regardless of what he said I flung myself around as per normal as instinct took over. Dave Ewing took me to one side and told me to just do my job and leave it at that. It was a sound piece of advice.

I wasn't the only one to be alienated by Saunders, whose tough, nononsense approach had found little support in the dressing room. In my view he was the wrong man in the wrong place at the wrong time. Ultimately, player power won the day and after the way he'd treated me, I shed no tears at his demise. Several key members of the squad had a meeting and then spoke to Peter Swales. They made it clear in the bluntest possible manner that they wanted Saunders out, saying they couldn't work with him, and eventually, after a 3–0 defeat at QPR, he was sacked on 11 April 1974. There was an enormous sense of relief in the dressing room and at least the chairman had been big enough to admit he'd brought the wrong man in. In later years Saunders would guide Aston Villa to European Cup glory so his methods were obviously effective; just not with us.

It was around this time that I was brought crashing down to earth again by, of all people, a director's wife. I'd been playing reserve-team football as we approached the end of the season and I was asked if, after the match, I'd go to the Blue Room – the press and photographers' bar at Maine Road – to attend a children's birthday party. It was the kid of one of our directors, Mr Cousins, and his wife introduced me in the following way: 'Children, this is Joe Corrigan. Unfortunately, our real goalkeeper is away playing with the first team.' My jaw, still sore, hit the floor and it made me wonder what her husband had been saying about me. To sap my confidence even further, there was a testimonial for Johnny Hart at Maine Road not long after and I was to play for one half and Bert Trautmann for the other. Bert played the first half and was enjoying himself so he asked to carry on after the break. I was quite happy with this arrangement; he was a club legend and everyone was delighted to see him back in goal for City.

I was asked midway through the second half to walk around to Bert to check he was okay and to ask if he wanted to come off, but, as I walked around the cinder track, I came in for dog's abuse from the City fans. 'You're useless Corrigan, you fat bastard,' someone shouted. 'Why don't you just fuck off? You're not fit to lace Bert's boots.' It hurt. At times like that you wondered why you bothered because it was hard to see a time when I'd win over the supporters. I should have ignored the heckling and given them the V-sign, but that wasn't my style. By this time I'd put most of my weight back on but it didn't feel as good as it had when I'd been a stone or so lighter. In consequence, I lost the weight again quickly by cutting down on potatoes – despite the fact that I loved steak and chips to the point of obsession – and was soon flying again in training. I knew that to be at my peak, fourteen stone was about my ideal weight.

Tony Book, still a player, was the popular choice in the dressing room to replace Saunders and he was given the job with four matches to go. It was just his luck that the first two games were, bizarrely, against Liverpool, but, for the last two, he recalled me for the matches against West Ham and Manchester United. Booky told me he was giving me a chance and to make sure I took it. We beat West Ham 2–1 and then travelled to Old Trafford for a game that would relegate United if we won. It was an intimidating atmosphere, with almost 60,000 fans packed into the ground, and there was real menace in the air. I knew something was going to happen, I just wasn't sure what.

Hooliganism was rife in English football and United fans had a reputation as bad as any club, but it was the first time I felt safe at a game just because I had a net behind me. It was goalless with minutes left and I was down at the Stretford End, so when Denis Law back-heeled the ball home in the most dramatic circumstances I knew what was coming. The United fans poured onto the pitch and I was surrounded within seconds, but I knew the safest place for me was to stay in my goal. Nobody could get to me from the back and if they wanted to have a go, they'd have to come at me from the front and from there I'd take my chances. There were thousands of United fans on the pitch in a vain attempt to get the game abandoned. A few of them tried to attack me but eventually five or six policemen arrived and formed a circle around my goal before escorting me back to the tunnel. It was a frightening experience and it could have been even uglier. In the end I was just happy to get back to the relative safety of the changing rooms. All the lads were there, except Denis, who had stripped off and was in the bath on his own, lost in thought. The referee decided not to take the teams back out and the result was later allowed to stand, but I wondered how the poor City fans were faring as they made their way home from Old Trafford. God help them, was all I could think at the time.

9

Rebirth of the Blue

I was glad to see the back of the 1973/74 season for a number of reasons. It had been a very unsettling year with three changes of manager, injuries, the arrival of Keith MacRae and a generally disappointing season for the team and supporters. I'd made just fifteen starts, my worst return since breaking into the team in 1969. I was no longer one of the kids, either. I was a senior member of the squad with nearly two hundred appearances under my belt.

Like anybody else, I had ambitions and wanted to play for England one day so my time playing reserve-team football had to come to an end. The only alternative was to leave City and to further my career elsewhere, which, considering recent events, might have been the best solution all round. Questions had been asked and fingers pointed as to why things had gone poorly the previous season and most of those fingers were pointing in my direction yet again. Sometimes I just thought: 'what's the point of being a footballer?' I had my dream job but it was making me unhappy. The chances of me becoming a pro had been so minimal, and the chances of me enjoying playing for one of the best teams in Europe and representing my country at under-twenty-three level had been even slimmer, yet there I was, the butt of everyone's jokes and a constant scapegoat for anything that went pear-shaped.

Still, I trained hard and took Keith's arrival as a spur because I wanted to prove I was better than he was. There was the knock-on effect that if I didn't dislodge him, it would be twice as hard to get a decent move away while I was rotting away in the stiffs. Perhaps it was self-pity, but my family were suffering too and my mum and dad were getting it the neck all the time because we lived in a big Manchester United area and they still went out to work every day. I was depressed, drinking more than I should have done and was close to packing it in. The stop-start nature of my career had to end and I realised this would be a watershed season for me, one way or another.

The pivotal moment came after a testimonial game. Alex Stepney and Gordon Banks were at the dinner later on and I was sitting at the bar chatting, drowning my sorrows and telling them that I'd become disillusioned with the game. They both told me I needed to alter my mindset, stop feeling sorry for myself and never consider quitting football. They told me that, in goalkeeping terms, I was still a baby and needed to get my head together. I listened impassively to their advice because I thought it was easy for them to say. How could they know how I was feeling? They did of course because they had been through it themselves at some point – all goalkeepers go through difficult periods. It slowly sunk in that if these guys could turn it around and go on to become legends in the game, why couldn't I? Only the ones with real ability rode out the storm so I refocused and decided that it was all or nothing from here on in.

Rodney Marsh had been named as captain for the season, a move that I felt was a compromise by Tony Book, one designed to get more out of him. It was clever in many ways and Tony was already showing he wasn't afraid to make big decisions regardless of how they were received in the dressing room. There was further proof of Tony's steel when Franny Lee tried to negotiate a wage rise during the summer, testing the rookie manager's resolve. The end result was that Franny moved to Derby County. His departure left a huge hole in the side because players like him are irreplaceable; he still had fire in his belly and was a natural-born winner and I'd miss him around the place. Perhaps inevitably, Derby won the league title in Franny's first season with them.

I had my own future to worry about, though. I had two young daughters and a wife to feed and for all my efforts to impress Tony, I began the new campaign as number two to Keith. It was going to be a steep learning curve for Booky and I felt he tried to get the club back on track by implementing a lot of the things he'd learned from Joe and Malcolm. He had the squad's full support – we had demanded that he be given a chance – and he brought back a much-needed air of stability that had been sadly absent since Joe left. He wanted to return to the values that had been in place when he first arrived at the club and to get City back to playing good football and winning trophies again.

As for my new skipper, what can I say? Marshy was a law unto himself, but basically a good guy with a dash of the superstar. I wasn't sure he was the right man to take us forward as a team and I felt we needed a more stable character as captain. Though nobody came out and said as much, there was an undercurrent of resentment that this flash git from London who had been at the club for little more than a year had been handed the armband. Alan Oakes must have felt more than a little put out at being overlooked after so many years at City, while Doyley and Tommy Booth both had undoubted leadership qualities and maybe they would have given Rodney a platform to show what he was capable of. It was all the more odd considering Booky had been skipper for so many years and led the side with a calming, fatherly attitude. Could Rodney take on that role? I had my doubts.

Booky told us we all had a chance to play in his team, and that, as far as he was concerned, we were starting with a clean slate. I still felt there was pressure on him to play Keith because of the money the club had spent on him, but I knew Booky was an honourable man and if he felt I deserved the jersey, he'd give me it. Every week I trained as hard as I could and my sole target was to see my name on the team sheet come Friday afternoon. If it wasn't, I knew I'd have a reserve game to play and another chance to impress. In fact, playing reserve games on the same day the first-team played was a good thing to do, because, while there would be the disappointment of not being in the team, you'd still be playing football rather than twiddling your thumbs. Plus there were some wily old characters knocking around the Central League in those days, so you could still continue your education as a keeper at that level. There'd always be some gnarly striker with his best days behind him prepared to rough you up and take out his frustrations on you, but it was excellent grounding. In addition, if I could iron out any weaknesses at that level with only a few hundred people watching, by the time I won back my first-team spurs, I'd be ready to stake my claim and this time keep my place. If it didn't result in a recall, at least it gave scouts from other clubs a chance to watch me. I'd shifted my mental attitude to such an extent that I saw positives in everything and I knew at some point I'd get at least one last crack at re-establishing myself.

Keith remained in goal for the first twenty-two league games of the season until he picked up an injury, giving me the opportunity I'd been waiting for. We were at home to Wolves, shortly before Christmas 1974, and drew 0–0 before travelling to Anfield for our annual stuffing by Liverpool. Whenever I saw any of the Liverpool players at functions or international get-togethers in later years they'd always say that playing City was their Christmas present because they knew they'd roll over us every time. It was amazing how many thrashings they'd dished out to us over the years and this Boxing Day visit was no different as we went down 4–1. For my next game, I had my old mate Franny Lee to contend with as he returned with Derby County, who were firing on all cylinders under Brian Clough. He did little to boost my confidence that day and scored a twenty-five-yard screamer that gave me no chance, securing a 2–1 win for his new employers.

I was one of the last ones off the pitch at Maine Road and as I neared the tunnel I could hear the jeers from the stands. Surely the City fans weren't blaming me for Franny's goal? Yet that's exactly what a few hundred punters were doing, despite it being voted goal of the season a few months later. This time I just switched off and let them voice their opinion. I had long since made up my mind that I wasn't going to be intimated and in fact I just thought to myself that I would look for some of those faces again when the crowd stayed behind to clap me off for helping to win games. I played twice more during a draw with Sheffield United and in a 5–1 win over Newcastle at Maine Road. I thought I'd done enough to continue my run but Keith's return to fitness meant I was out in the cold again and we lost the next match 4–0 at Stoke City. The transfer deadline was approaching and I wondered if anything might happen, especially when the *Manchester Evening News* ran a story about which goalkeeper we were going to sign, with pictures of all the usual suspects: Phil Parkes, Jimmy Rimmer, in fact anybody else wearing gloves at the time. It was Groundhog Day, predictable journalism. If someone came in with a bid, I'd probably have gone, but then Keith tore a hamstring a few days before the March transfer deadline. Booky came up to me and said: 'Look, Joe, I'm not signing a new goalkeeper. I'll give you the opportunity to show me what you can do and you've got from now until the end of the season to show me what you are capable of. Go out and do it, son.'

I took no satisfaction that Keith was laid up with injury. It wasn't the way I wanted to win back my place but I knew this would probably be my last chance at City. There could be no fumbles, no errors of judgement and no nerves. I had the ability and I needed to focus and keep my concentration every time I went out; there was no other option. My first game would be away to QPR, and, bearing in mind what had happened at Burnley with Doyley some eighteen months before – the game that had almost ended my career with the Blues – I decided it was time to have a word with him and set the matter straight once and for all. The fact that I chose to do it as we made our way down the tunnel at Loftus Road might have surprised a few people but it was perfect timing. I was the biggest lad in the squad and it was time I used my presence to take command of my destiny. Nobody was going to take that green jersey off me, and, if anyone got in the way, I'd sort it out the only way I knew how. I got hold of Doyley by his shirt collars, pushed my face close to his and said:

'Don't ever do that to me again.'

'What are you talking about?' Doyley replied, genuinely bemused.

'Don't ever do it again. We all make mistakes.'

He knew exactly what I was talking about. It cleared the air between us and it felt good to finally get it off my chest. Doyley was a good pro and I think he respected what I'd done because it was the kind of thing he'd do himself. That was the end of the matter. We made our way on to the pitch and nothing more was said.

I still needed a slice of luck to tell me the gods were on my side, something to alter the City fans' perception of me. I still had a lot of work to do on that front as I discovered a week later when we played Coventry City. They were awarded a free kick in a dangerous position just outside my box. The ball was whipped in, and heading for the top corner, but I managed to scramble across and tip it over. It was a good save but it was greeted with ironic cheers by a fair number of City fans. I can't begin to express how much that hurt. I was willing them to give me one more chance but it seemed that I was some sort of liability who had had his chance. Yet I knew if I could get them on my side, there would be no turning back – and away to Wolves, three matches later, the tide finally began to turn in my favour.

I was up against two of the best strikers in the division that afternoon in the shape of John Richards and Derek Dougan and they were giving me a busy, bruising afternoon. I came out for a cross and was clattered by Dougan. The impact caused me to drop the ball and Richards knocked it in the net. The whistle blew and I thought, 'Oh, shit. Here we go again.' But as I looked up expecting to see the referee pointing to the centre circle, he was pointing instead for a foul on me. Twelve months previously and that would have been a goal and I would be to blame again, but this time it had gone my way. That one moment was the turning point in my career and from then on I got the little breaks I'd be hoping for. It may have seemed a relatively unimportant moment, but had it not been for that referee thinking I'd been fouled, it would have been all over. My confidence improved and I got better and better. It gave me the encouragement to look at every aspect of my game. I consulted a doctor and a dietician and went on a strict eating and drinking regime, losing a stone in weight. I didn't eat as much and what I did consume was more protein-based, cutting out potatoes and bread. I wasn't going to let this opportunity pass me by; if I failed, it wouldn't be for the lack of effort.

I kept my place for the remainder of the season and we ended it by flying out to Nigeria in early May to play Nigerian club Shooting Stars and a Nigerian military side. We went from Manchester to London and then on to Lagos and, as the stewardess opened the plane door, we were hit by intense blast of heat. The airport was on the edge of the desert and we'd never experienced anything like it. It was a time when Booky and Rodney Marsh were embroiled in a battle of wills that was, at times, quite amusing to watch. We were told to fly out in smart-casual dress but Rodney turned up in a three-piece suit with shirt and tie, but no socks. It was typical Rodney. While the plane was refuelled we went into the lounge, where there was only one huge electric fan, totally inadequate in the searing African temperatures. The sweat was pouring off us and Rodney was just sitting there in his suit and tie having a beer, making his own protest about Booky's dress code. He was visibly melting, but was too stubborn to buckle. The war of attrition had been smouldering all season, but you felt there could only be one winner – and it wasn't going to be Rodney. Booky had done what Malcolm hadn't when he became manager – and that was to distance himself from the players. He wasn't our teammate any more, he wasn't our drinking buddy; he was our manager and he wanted to stamp his authority on the team, which, in all fairness, he had to do. But Marshy just couldn't help himself and wasn't impressed by the change of attitude in the quiet, almost shy, man we'd all known as 'Skip'. The friction continued throughout the season. Booky was totally focused and that sometimes projected itself in what Rodney obviously perceived as a dour attitude. On one occasion he turned up for training wearing a specially printed T-shirt with 'Smile' across his chest. To his credit, Tony turned up with one of his own a couple of days later, with 'Play' printed on it.

Rodney then bought a brand new Mini and had had 'Smile' painted on the bodywork. It wasn't the best way to build a harmonious attitude in the squad; this was the manager and the captain when all is said and done. Although the digs being exchanged seemed harmless, and were often amusing, the situation could only deteriorate. Some years later, Rodney told me in a bar in Fort Lauderdale that he felt let down that the team didn't back his efforts to get Tony to lighten up. But I'd just got back into the side and younger players like Willie Donachie needed to stay on the fence. We had our own careers to worry about and saw it as a clash of personalities that we could do nothing about.

We played our two tour games and headed home again to rest up for the summer. Had I done enough to retain my place for the new season? I thought I had. In my mind, I'd turned the corner and from there on, I aimed to enjoy every minute of being City's number one and I knew that if my name was on the team-sheet for the opening game of the 1975/76 season, the shirt would be mine for keeps, so to speak.

10

England Expects

Dennis Tueart was proving a terrific signing for us. He'd joined just after the 1974 League Cup final defeat to Wolves and had settled in quickly. He was a great finisher and it wasn't long before he was hugely popular on the terraces. Booky was beginning to shape the team in his own image and had added Asa Hartford and Dave Watson to the squad and was bringing through youngsters such as Kenny Clements, Paul Power, Ged Keegan, Gary Owen and Ken Barnes's lad, Peter. Joe Royle arrived with Watson in time for the 75/76 season, and, looking at the squad on paper, I thought we had a real chance of winning something. It might be a year or so too soon to challenge Liverpool for the title, but there was real potential and Booky deserved a lot of credit for completely rebuilding the team without a lot of fuss. Buzzer had gone leaving only Colin Bell as the surviving member of the trio the fans had dubbed the Holy Trinity. While Franny and Buzzer's influence on the team had diminished slightly as time went on, Colin's had, if anything, grown stronger. With his relentless drive, anything was possible.

Much to my relief I began as first choice for the opening game of the season, at home to Norwich, and, with Keith fit again, I knew I had the edge over him. Despite the talent in the team, Marshy, in my view, was still proving disruptive. I also thought he was much less effective when things were going badly; I remember one time after we played QPR that our coach Ian McFarlane tried to lay into him because of what he saw as

Marsh's lacklustre performance and the players having to break them up. Just as well for Rodney because Ian would have pulverised him. Rodney played for the opening dozen games before he was finally dropped after an abject display against Burnley and was also stripped of the captaincy; given everything that had happened I think Booky had given up the ghost as far as Marsh was concerned. Mike Doyle took the armband and it would turn out that Rodney had played his final game for the club on that fateful afternoon against the Clarets. That situation would linger for several months as the club tried to offload him for well under his market value. However, the Marsh sideshow was about to be overshadowed by the loss of Colin Bell to one of the worst tackles I've ever seen.

It was during a League Cup tie against United at Maine Road and I was right in line with Colin as he burst towards the Reds' goal with typical determination. I saw Martin Buchan scythe him down with what looked to me like a disgusting challenge, as Colin pushed the ball to go past him. Right away we all knew it was serious and everyone was devastated. Colin was taken straight to hospital, where I was later told that a syringe used to drain the blood behind the knee blew the needle out of the joint such was the pressure in his leg. We could never replace him and I believe it cost the team countless trophies during the Seventies when we often came so close to glory. Had Colin been playing, we'd have been a match for Liverpool and quite possibly have been the team of the decade. I honestly felt that the team Tony Book had assembled had the potential to be even better than the one Joe and Malcolm built, but only with Colin fit and flying. He could do everything – create, tackle, score goals and was simply irreplaceable for both club and country. His knee had effectively been destroyed and it seemed his career was over. We had to push on without him, though you can never be the same team having lost a player of his stature.

On a personal level, I still felt the fans weren't totally with me, though the boo-boys were not as vocal as they had been. I'd only turn that around by consistent performances on the pitch and I knew I was doing the business now, so I hoped it was just a matter of time.

Booky's first-team coach was Ian MacFarlane, a great character and an excellent coach, very knowledgeable and experienced but a fiery Scot with a terrible temper. The lads thought the world of him and I recall one occasion when he picked up Ged Keegan and I from our homes in

City versus Everton, August 1968. Playing at Maine Road was always so special, especially for a twenty-year-old rookie keeper.
(courtesy PA Photos)

Family matters.
This is me, age three, with my sister
Bernadette, who was then a year old.

Val and I get engaged, 1969

From left to right: Val, my son Andrew and my daughters Sara and Emma.

Learning from the master: while on loan to Shrewsbury Town manager Harry Gregg took me under his wing. The Manchester United legend became the biggest influence on my career.

Christmas pantomime, 1971. We always had such a laugh in the early days at City, which wasn't hard in these costumes! The panto was held in the supporters club building next to Maine Road and the stars are (*from left to right*) Booky, yours truly, Buzzer and Franny.

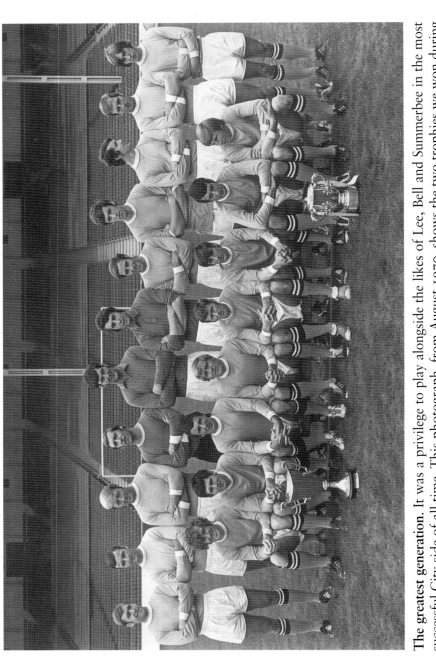

The greatest generation. It was a privilege to play alongside the likes of Lee, Bell and Summerbee in the most successful City side of all time. This photograph, from August 1970, shows the two trophies we won during the previous season: the League Cup and the European Cup Winners Cup. (*courtesy Getty Images Ltd*)

City keepers.

Having to follow in the footsteps of legendary keepers like Frank Swift and Bert Trautmann (*pictured*) made it even harder for me as a young player. But Bert was always very generous to me with his time and his advice.

In 1973 Keith MacRae was signed for a world-record fee (for a goalkeeper) and I faced a real battle to regain my place as number one at Maine Road. *(courtesy Getty Images Ltd)*

Hard training sessions at Platt Lane helped me win my place back in the first team and to retain it for many years.

With my favourite comedian – a true Blue – Bernard Manning.

In 1976 I was delighted to receive the first of my three player-of-the-year awards from City supporters. Gary Owen (with trophies) won the young-player award.

My greatest save. I somehow managed to push this header from Allan Clarke of Leeds United round the post during a cup tie at Elland Road in 1977. A good friend, Tudor Thomas, gave me a painting of the save and it hangs in my living room to this day.

In the San Siro, 1978. It was a great feeling to walk out into this wonderful stadium for a UEFA Cup tie. Even better, we knocked the Italian giants out to progress to the quarter-final of the competition.

Derby day. I always looked forward to our jousts with Man Utd and enjoyed a lot of success against them. In this instance I was glad to see Steve Coppell's shot cannon off the post.
(courtesy PA Photos)

The triumvirate, 1980. I was up against Peter Shilton (*left*) and Ray Clemence, two of the greatest keepers in history, for a place in the England team. But I still believe that I should have won more caps for my country. *(courtesy Mirrorpix)*

England Football Senior Squad, 1979.

England squad. It is such an honour to pull on that 'Three Lions' shirt, even if I was often confined to the bench during matches.

Turning points

In my view, the signing of Rodney Marsh in early 1972 disrupted the team's rhythm and cost us the league title that year.
(courtesy PA Photos)

Joe Mercer (*right*) and Malcolm Allison were a potent management team in the late Sixties and early Seventies, as their record proves. But Malcolm struggled badly after Joe left City, missing his steady hand on the tiller, and was effectively forced to leave the club in 1973.
(courtesy Getty Images Ltd)

In arguably the worst decision in the club's history Malcolm was brought back to the club in 1979, as 'coaching overlord'. Although Tony Book (*left*) was still officially the manager, it was Allison who pulled the strings. It would all end in tears. *(courtesy Getty Images Ltd)*

Wembley.
I look a bit shell-shocked but City had just beaten Newcastle to win the 1976 League Cup final. I am being congratulated by coach Ian McFarlane.

City reached the 1981 FA Cup final where we faced Spurs. After a 2–2 draw in the first game we lost the replay 3–2. Many consider these games the most thrilling in FA Cup history and while I was delighted to be named man of the match in both I would have gladly traded this honour for a winner's medal. I am shown here making a save in the first game.

Leaving City
I was very sad to leave the club I loved after seventeen years but was
honoured to receive a parting gift from Junior Blues chairman Tony Miles.

I was touched that many Blues fans took the trouble to come to
the airport to wish me luck with my new club, Seattle Sounders.
They included the legendary Big Helen Turner, pictured here with her
famous cow bell.

My time in the States with the Sounders was cut short by the financial problems suffered by the North American Soccer League (NASL).

The team behind the team. I enjoyed ten great years at Anfield as coach
and assistant manager. My time at Liverpool included winning the
UEFA Cup against Alves of Spain in 2001. The coaching colleagues
celebrating that victory are (*from left to right*) Sammy Lee,
Patrice Bergues, Phil Thompson, Gerard Houllier and me.

As well as being goalkeeper coach I managed the reserve team at Anfield for a spell. Here we are after winning the FA Premier League title.

Practice makes perfect. This montage – taken during one training session at Cheadle in 1978 – shows just what we keepers have to go through. You really do have to be mad to be a goalie.

Sale and gave us a lift to training. We were driving along what is now the M60 towards Cheadle when Ian turned to me and said, 'I can't believe it, big man. When Malcolm Allison was coach of this team, they gave him a Jaguar to drive and all I get is a bloody Cortina.' He looked at Ged in his rear-view mirror and asked, 'What did you think of Malcolm as a coach, son? Do you think he was better than me?'

Ged swallowed and said, 'Well, I don't think so, Ian.'

Ian glanced over at me. 'What about you, big man? Was he a better coach than me?'

I began by saying, 'Well . . .' but I didn't get to finish my sentence because Ian slammed his brakes on in the middle lane of the motorway! Cars were flying past on both sides and how one didn't plough into the back of us, I'll never know. He was scowling at me as cars whizzed by at speed, sounding their horns.

'Okay, okay,' I quickly conceded, 'you're a better coach than Malcolm.'

'Right you are, big man,' he said, and we continued our journey. What a character!

There was another telling incident when we played at the Baseball Ground in 1976. Out of sheer frustration I had kicked the ball into the crowd and it hit a Derby supporter full in the face. After the match the irate fan stormed down the tunnel and tried to get into our dressing room to sort me out. Unfortunately for him the doorway was blocked by Ian, who, without further ado, landed a beautiful right hook on the man's jaw, knocking him onto his backside. After two blows to the head in quick succession he might have concluded it just wasn't his day.

Later that season, we reached the League Cup final and after the last two seasons I'd had, it was a real thrill to be involved. Dennis Tueart and I used to do our own pre-match warm-up before matches and we continued that at Wembley. Dennis buried a shot past me and as I went into the net to retrieve the ball another ball almost took my head off. I looked up to see who it was and there was big Ian running around Wembley as though he'd scored the winner in the final. I asked him in the changing rooms what he'd been up to and he said, 'I've always wanted to score against England at Wembley, big man. Bloody fantastic feeling.'

Having made my first appearance at Wembley on a mud bath of a pitch, it was lovely to walk out with the rest of the team on to the bowling-green surface that had made it the most wonderful football venue in the world.

The sun was shining, we felt great and the 2–1 win over Newcastle was thoroughly deserved, with Tueart's winner out of this world. He reminded me so much of Denis Law when he was a youngster; as an instinctive finisher with two great feet Tueart had it all. With thirty seconds to go of that game there was another example of how my luck had changed. A Newcastle corner came over and I mistimed my punch and the ball ended up in the six-yard box instead of outside the area as I'd intended, but as it fell to a Newcastle player I managed to block the shot and the ball was cleared up field – such was the thin dividing line between success and failure. I'd have been hard pressed to live down a howler in a Wembley cup final.

It was an incredible day, the icing on the cake. I finished the campaign having played in all but one of the forty-two league games and our final placing of eighth was a decent effort. I felt, for want of a better word, cleansed and after two-and-a-half years of abuse, self-doubt and patchy form I was relaxed and confident in my own ability, which, in turn, showed in my performances. I'd done the right thing by keeping my head down, losing weight and working hard; as the saying goes you reap what you sow. I wondered where I stood with the City fans and soon found out when I was voted the supporters' player of the year, winning comfortably I believe. I'd received vindication from the City supporters, who recognised that I'd fought hard to be first choice and I was a much better all-round keeper than I'd been a couple of seasons before. They knew I'd battled hard to win their respect and I was absolutely delighted – an understatement, in fact – but I wasn't about to move into the comfort zone. It had taken a monumental effort to get to that stage and I wasn't about to let complacency creep in. I had to keep improving for club and country. I was entering a whole new chapter of my career at Maine Road and I was determined to enjoy it to the full.

And things were about to get even better.

The club had planned an end-of-season tour of Japan and South Korea. I was really looking forward to the trip, which would take in seven games over a three-week period. We'd be playing the Japanese national team four times and the South Koreans three times. Having never been to that part of the world, I was eager to experience a different culture as well as do a bit of sightseeing in Tokyo. A week before we were due to fly out England played Scotland at Hampden Park and Ray Clemence let a shot from Kenny Dalglish trickle through his legs and into the net. My thoughts were 'there but for the grace of God . . .' and I knew how Ray must have felt at that moment. Shortly after the match, I received a letter from the FA advising me that I'd been selected for England's tour of North America, following Peter Shilton's withdrawal. I had to pinch myself that this was really happening and after getting my gear together at extremely short notice, I travelled down to London to join the squad. The England squad had been together for several days after competing in the home internationals and were all set for the tour. My late arrival meant I had to wear a suit that had been tailored to fit somebody else – not that easy when you're six foot five and nearly fifteen stones. Let's just say there was the odd mention of half-mast trousers on the flight over. Shilton's decision not to tour was because he'd been unhappy at being number two to Clemence in recent matches. I didn't agree with his stance. When you are asked to play for your country, you accept the invitation because there is no higher honour and if the manager thinks another man can do a better job, you have to respect his decision. Shilton inspired me as a keeper, but his attitude often disappointed me, even though, indirectly, I had him to thank for my first senior call-up.

I have to admit, I always thought Clemence was the better keeper of the two; he was a fantastic natural athlete, a good kicker of the ball and had great powers of concentration. Shilton too had many attributes: he had wonderful reflexes, he was a good organiser and he had a tremendous work ethic. If there was one area that let him down it was dealing with crosses deep to the far post; I felt this was because the severe weight-training programme he had been on made him too rigid and inflexible. Shilts and I used to work our arses off for both club and country, whereas Clem trained when he had to, did just enough and no more. But when he played for either Liverpool or England, he was outstanding – even if he had nothing to do for eighty-nine minutes, he could produce a world-class save out of nowhere in the ninetieth. I must add, despite my admiration for both men, I felt I was not only better than both of them, but also by then the best in the world, and nothing will change that opinion.

We all had admiration and respect for one another's ability and realised that we were in a privileged position being in the England squad, especially with so many other talented goalies around during the Seventies. Experience had taught me that anything can happen at any time and

Shilton was missing the bigger picture by sulking. If Clemence had picked up an injury, he'd have been given the jersey, but that was his choice, not mine. Considering I'd been on the verge of quitting a couple of years before, it made me think back to my chat with Gordon Banks and Alex Stepney, who I hoped would have wry smiles on their faces when they learned of my call-up. My dad was ever so proud and it was a pity that we were so far away and he couldn't come along to watch, but he had a few beers at his local when he heard the news.

I was still a little awestruck when we flew out to Los Angeles. I'd always wanted to go to America, but to travel as part of an England squad was a dream come true. The first game was against Brazil at the Coliseum in Los Angeles. I was on the bench as a kind of unused sub, but it was an incredible occasion and to see the likes of Rivelino up close in the flesh will stay with me forever.

I discovered on that trip that England manager Don Revie had some interesting bonding methods, such as putting on competitions and bingo, all aimed at creating a sense of camaraderie. I was the third-choice keeper behind Clemence and Jimmy Rimmer, but the training sessions were an education and it was great to work with Clem and Jimmy on a daily basis. Then it was off to Tarrytown, Westchester County, in the sate of New York, where we would be based for several days, commuting to New York City for the game against Italy. We went into Manhattan for an official dinner near Central Park, with, it was hoped, a bit of sightseeing to come later. After we'd eaten, a few of us wanted to have a look around but the commissionaire wouldn't allow us to leave because we had our England blazers on and he felt we'd be sitting ducks for any undesirables who might be hanging around. With the reputation certain areas of New York had back then, it was probably for the best.

The match against Italy was played at Yankee Stadium, and it was filled with 45,000 fanatical Italians. We went in at the break 2–0 down and me and a few of the other subs went out for a kick around to sample the atmosphere and keep ourselves warmed up. Then England coach Les Cocker ran across to me and said, 'You'd better come back in, Joe – you're playing.' I thought he was joking and told him as much, but he insisted I went back to the changing rooms to prepare. I jogged back in to find Don Revie waiting. He said, 'Get ready, you are going on now, son.'

Jimmy Rimmer, who had started in goal, was substituted and that forty-five minutes would be his only England cap. I heard that Revie just didn't fancy him as an England keeper and decided to use the chance to give me a run out instead of persevering with Rimmer. Whether Jimmy did himself a disservice, I don't know, but he rubbed one or two people up the wrong way with his slightly eccentric behaviour during that tour. He was a very superstitious man and didn't want to wear the official England shirt, tie and blazer, preferring his own gear because he felt it brought him luck. Don Revie did things by the book, so Jimmy's dress code was never going to impress him. Everything was meticulously planned and I think Jimmy's decision to wear his own suit didn't go down too well.

Whatever the reasons, I was now representing England against Italy in New York and it doesn't get any better than that. There was however one problem: Yankee Stadium is a baseball park, home to the world-famous New York Yankees, and hardly conducive to attractive soccer, as the Americans call our national game. To my surprise I discovered that one corner of my penalty area was the pitcher's mound! Strikers didn't know whether to score a goal or hit a home run. I couldn't have cared less if we'd have played on a cabbage patch because I was on cloud nine. We battled back to lead 3–2, and, with minutes remaining, I came out for a cross and an Italian striker gave me a right wallop as I managed to scramble the ball away. I turned around to see Mick Mills fighting with the Italian and Dave Clement and I both got involved as the fists flew in the goalmouth.

There was one more game on the tour and that was against Team America, a side picked from the best players in the North American Soccer League. Among their number were Pele and former Liverpool hard man Tommy Smith. My roommate, Ray Clemence, had been recalled for that game, which we won 4–1, but it had been an amazing experience and a fantastic tour to be involved with. For me, the shackles were off and the self-doubt was cast aside. I was an England international now and the sky was the limit.

There was no turning back.

11

My Greatest Save

Many people have asked me over the years when my friendship with Helen Turner – 'Big Helen' as everybody at Maine Road knew her – began in earnest. Helen, who sat directly behind the goal in the north stand, was probably City's most famous supporter. Her unique way of geeing up the players and fans, by ringing her Swiss cowbell, became part of Manchester City folklore.

My first dealings with her date from March 1975, when I broke back into the side at QPR. I've always been superstitious and there were certain rituals I adhered to on match days, but, at Loftus Road that day, I was about to start another. Just before the game, as we warmed up, Helen shouted me over from her seat among the City contingent. She handed me a sprig of heather and said, 'This is for good luck.' I took it, and, though we lost 1–0, nothing unfortunate happened during the game, a bonus for me during a period in which I had some wretched luck. For the next game, at home to Carlisle, she gave me another sprig, and, though we lost 2–1, I played well. I always put the heather in a little pocket in my goalkeeper's glove bag inside the nets and I kept every sprig she gave me in a plastic bag at home until the end of the season.

I recall one occasion that Helen turned up late to a game, against Leicester City, and I didn't manage to get my heather in time; I let a ball go through my legs and into the net. That reinforced the theory that Helen's gift was keeping the demons at bay – either mine or otherwise!

I was so superstitious that if I began the season with a good game I would wear the same clothes on the day of each match, from the same tie right down to the same socks, because I honestly believed – and still do – that in some way it helped. I'd take my ring, watch and chain off in the same order before a match and place them in the same pocket and suchlike. Whether it made a difference, I don't suppose we'll ever know, but it helped me psychologically and that did matter.

The 1976/77 season was memorable in so many ways and it was also the year when the City fans finally got right behind me. It had begun with the disappointing loss of first-team coach Ian MacFarlane during the close season, a man I'd miss not only for his expertise on the training pitch, but also as a person. You can't lose someone like that and not feel sad, but he had his reasons, personal rather than football, and had left the club. I have a lot of good memories of working with Ian, but one that sticks in my mind was the day I called round to his house and he and his wife had just had a major barney about decorating. He asked me to give him a hand and his wife later explained why. Ian had wall-papered the lounge a few days before and gone to bed happy with his efforts. When Mrs MacFarlane came down in the morning, however, every strip of paper had fallen off and was littered around the room. She wasn't best pleased.

He was an intense character; hot-headed, yet loveable. Television presenter Stuart Hall once came down to film a feature for BBC 1's *Look North West* prior to the 1976 League Cup final. We were at Cheadle training, and, as the crew began filming us, Ian and Tony Book, who had been involved in a heated five-a-side game, began exchanging blows after a clash. It was both comical and embarrassing to see our manager and assistant manager fighting a few days before a showpiece final when we were supposed to transmit an air of harmony. There was no malice in it but it typified Ian's passion.

After the final, we were at a reception in London and Ian stood up to say a few words and mentioned a situation involving him moving house and his problems obtaining a bridging loan from the club. He told us he probably wouldn't be with City the following season, and, being a man of principle, he most likely gave the board an ultimatum and stood by it when it became clear there was no help forthcoming. His replacement could not have been better; the club announced that England coach Bill

Taylor was going to be Tony Book's right-hand man. I already knew that Bill, another Scot, was a tremendous coach from my summer tour with England and I hoped he would help me move to the next level over the next few years. He made simple observations that made such a big difference to me, with arguably his best idea being a training session on the morning of a match. 'You're a goalkeeper; you're not going to have much to do during the game so why not train in the morning beforehand? It'll tell you all you need to know about the ground and conditions,' he argued.

'What if we're away?' I asked.

'Then we train in the grounds of the hotel.'

It seemed like a good plan to me, so I began a routine in which I'd have breakfast and then go out with Bill for about forty-five minutes before returning to prepare for the match. If there was no pitch to train on, we'd put a few coats down and use them for goals, just as kids do in the park. I'd dive around and Bill would fire a variety of shots at me. It gave me an edge and I followed this practice for the rest of my career. I'd train on the same patch of ground at Maine Road every week and groundsman Stan Gibson would go mad with me for churning up a patch of his perfect playing surface. A creature of habit I never moved spots, much to his chagrin.

We began the campaign with real belief that we could challenge for the title, strange as that might sound considering we'd finished eighth the previous season. All the pieces of Tony Book's jigsaw seemed to fit perfectly, apart from the absence of Colin Bell. Few if any of the lads believed he could come back from such a crippling knee injury and, mentally, we prepared thinking he wouldn't be taking part in the season ahead. We'd miss his twenty-odd goals a season, assists and all-round energy, but the lad was doing everything he could to work his way back to fitness. The odds were stacked against him, though, and his knee just didn't look right. It was heartbreaking to watch such a talent ruined by what I thought had been recklessness, but we had to press on.

We lost just one of our opening eight league and cup matches, five of which I kept clean sheets in. Having not done anything of note in Europe since reaching the Cup Winners Cup semi-final in 1971, our League Cup triumph in 1976 (Aston Villa dumped us out in the first round of this season) meant we were in the UEFA Cup and we were confident of a good run. That is until the draw was made, pitting us against tournament favourites Juventus. We won the first leg 1–0, but the second leg in Turin was always going to be tough because Juve had a world-class squad. It was the first time I'd come up against a team that would do anything to come out on top. Their win-at-all-costs attitude resulted in cynical challenges, time-wasting, shirt tugging, you name it. Juventus had mastered every trick in the book and while I don't think ability necessarily won the day, experience and gamesmanship just edged it their way.

One challenge summed up their philosophy perfectly. A cross came in from the right and as Tommy Booth leapt to head the ball clear Marco Tardelli launched himself horizontally at Tommy and clattered him on the back. The challenge could easily have broken Tommy's spine so I grabbed hold of Tardelli, who was theatrically protesting his innocence. Meanwhile Freddie Griffiths, our physio, ran on to treat Tom, who had two sets of stud marks down the length of his back. I was pulled away before I chinned him and that's when I noticed the Juventus players had an intense look in their eye, a look that said defeat just wasn't an option. They did a very professional job on us and won 2–0, eventually going on to win the competition.

At international level I was included in the England squad for the game against Finland in Helsinki and was on the bench alongside Jimmy Rimmer, but neither of us played. With Peter Shilton claiming prior to the tour of North America that if he wasn't going to be England's first choice he didn't want to play any more, both Jimmy and I felt there was a real chance to become second choice behind Clem. Yet after the Finland game, and despite what I thought were churlish comments, Shilts was selected again by Don Revie, which meant I was sent to watch from the stand. I can't put into words how much this upset me; I would have crawled over broken glass to play for England. If he felt he was too good to be on the bench, his place should have gone to people who were honoured to be there, even as squad members. Revie backed down when he could have taught Shilton a lesson and that surprised and disappointed me given his strict disciplinary record at Leeds.

Like I said, that should have been it for him; once you say no to England, I strongly feel the door should be closed in your face. To my mind Shilts had spat his dummy out and had got his own way whereas I had to work bloody hard for my chances and couldn't understand why, when he turned his back, they didn't select me. Looking at the hugely successful club sides Shilts and Clem played for in Nottingham Forest and Liverpool respectively, I admit it crossed my mind more than once that if I'd played my football at either of those teams, or even at Manchester United or Arsenal, I would have won more caps than the solitary one I had up to that point. Certainly, that would have been true in seasons to come.

Of course, I was unfortunate to be around at a time when there were two world-class goalkeepers ahead of me for England and if I'd qualified for Scotland or Wales, I might have been a seasoned international at that stage in my career. In fact, a relative of my dad's – a parish priest from County Roscommon in Ireland – had enquired prior to my cap against Italy whether I would qualify to represent Ireland because my grandparents were both Irish. Father Tom travelled to Dublin and lobbied for a rule change, but UEFA's approval would have been required and there was so much red tape to cut through that it was always unlikely to happen. My appearance for the England under-twenty-three side against Russia in 1969 meant I was ineligible – which, of course, isn't the case today – but that was the end of the matter. Ronnie Healey went on to play for Ireland and won more caps for Ireland than I did for England and good luck to him – maybe he saw the writing on the wall. Still, football is all about opinions and the plain fact of the matter was that the England manager, rightly or wrongly, believed Ray Clemence and Peter Shilton had the edge on me. As I said earlier, it wasn't what I believed, but, in truth, after the way things had gone for me at club level in previous years, I was just happy to be part of a very good City team. Playing for England was a massive bonus.

In the league we were going really well, losing just two of our first twenty-five games and remaining unbeaten from late October until mid-February. It was a fantastic run and one game sticks in my mind more than most: a 2–0 win at Leeds United, not for the result, which was rare, but because the events that led up to it left me in a state of shock for several days. Two days before we faced Leeds we had been enjoying a low-key party on Boxing Day 1976 when Dave Cocker, a very close friend of mine, nipped across the road to his house to get a few cans of beer. After a short while, his wife Sue asked me where I thought he was and I told her he had gone home for a few cans. I wanted to leave it for five minutes but she was worried, so I said I'd go and get him. I went into his house, but he didn't answer when I shouted. There was a light on upstairs and I went up to the bathroom; the door was ajar and there on the floor was Dave. I didn't know if he'd passed out or what the problem was, but within a few seconds I knew he was dead. I tried to resuscitate him, but it was hopeless. He'd had a massive heart attack and nothing could be done. It was a terrible shock because it had come completely without warning. The next day we travelled to Elland Road and I must have been on autopilot because I can't recall anything from the game. It made me realise just how fragile life is.

We returned to Elland Road for a fifth-round FA Cup tie and we all felt that we could repeat the Boxing Day win and then go on and win the trophy. We played well but Leeds were slightly better on the day, although I made arguably the greatest save of my career. A cross came in from the left and Allan Clarke was waiting at the far post to nod the ball home. He made a great connection but I managed to twist in midair and palm the ball out at the foot of the post before Doyley knocked it away. Tudor Thomas, who would later chair my testimonial committee, gave me a painting of the save, which hangs proudly in my lounge to this day. Trevor Cherry later scored the only goal of the game to leave us concentrating on the league. We were neck and neck with Liverpool going into the spring, but narrow defeats at West Ham and Bristol City held us back, and a 2–1 loss at Anfield meant we couldn't afford to drop any more points in the run-in. We won our next three games after Liverpool before travelling to the Baseball Ground to take on Derby County, a team that had beaten us on their own patch for the past five seasons. We knew, with just five games to go, that this would be a pivotal game in our bid to be champions, but it turned out a complete disaster.

It began badly and ended in utter chaos on a pitch that would have been better suited to kids with buckets and spades. Our misery would be compounded by a brilliant little Scotsman, Archie Gemmill, who was magnificent. An incident from that day resulted in my appearance on BBC Two's cult show *Fantasy Football*, with David Baddiel and Frank Skinner, which I'll come to in a moment. Derby were already ahead when they were awarded a second-half penalty. There was only one problem: the state of the pitch meant there was no penalty spot. The ball was placed where the referee assumed the spot should be, but if there's one thing a goalkeeper is sure of, it's when the ball is even a fraction too close and I felt it was well off the mark. I protested to the referee, marching twelve paces to place the ball where I felt the spot should be. The referee wasn't impressed and booked me – then he asked for a tape measure! You couldn't have scripted it. The distance was measured and this guy in a garish, chequered suit with huge lapels appeared with a bucket of white paint and a brush and began to paint a penalty spot. Later, on *Match of the Day*, Jimmy Hill proved that I'd been correct in my assumption and got the distance spot-on, so to speak. Nevertheless I got four disciplinary points for ungentlemanly conduct, four more points that we managed as a team having left Derby with a 4–0 thrashing, even though we hadn't actually merited such a heavy loss.

Skinner and Baddiel's recreation of this bizarre afternoon, for the 'Phoenix from the Flames' section of their show, was filmed some twenty or so years later in a park in London. It ended with me taking the bucket to measure out the spot but after a dozen paces I just kept walking into the distance. It was a good laugh and helped exorcise the memory of the game. For the record, Derby converted the penalty.

The defeat at Derby severely dented our confidence and we never recovered, despite winning two and drawing two of the remaining games, one of which was against Everton in our final home game of the season. It was during this game that, regrettably, I lost my rag with City midfielder Gary Owen and did exactly the same thing Mike Doyle had done to me in 1973. I should have known better. Gary was a young kid and he gave the ball away on the edge of the box allowing Everton to equalise. Enraged, I ran out and picked him up, shouting, 'You little bastard! What did you think you were doing?' I was totally out of order and I apologised to him after the match, but I think my frustration at losing the title, which that result guaranteed, just got to me.

Our final-day win at Coventry City meant we finished a point behind Liverpool and even today I feel we were better than them that season; they just had the experience of knowing where the title could be won and lost. For us, defeats at Ashton Gate, Upton Park and the Baseball Ground cost us dearly, though with a fit Colin Bell I am sure the title would have ended up at Maine Road rather than Anfield.

As for me, the season ended on a high for two reasons. Firstly I was selected to play in a Football League side to play a Glasgow Select at Hampden Park to commemorate the Queen's silver jubilee. I met Her

Majesty that day, too, which was a personal honour. If my hands were shaking a little when we were introduced, it wasn't nerves – just the fact I'd nearly been involved in a plane crash at Manchester Airport earlier that day. We'd boarded the aircraft, were prepared to take-off and everything seemed perfectly normal. But as we picked up speed the plane suddenly veered violently off the runway. Seconds later a plane landed in the spot we'd just left. I know what I saw and I know we all had a narrow escape, though I think it went unreported in the press with the airport seemingly intent on something of a cover-up. I am thankful that I lived to fight another day.

I didn't think anything could top meeting the Queen, but it wasn't the case. First I was voted the supporters' player of the year for a second successive season and then my only son Andrew was born on 24 July 1977, and, just as it was with the girls, I was over the moon because he was born strong and healthy and Val was just fine, too. We'd been really worried because she had contracted chicken pox during the pregnancy and so we were mightily relieved when we were told by the midwife he was fine. There was one thing Val and I had agreed on: that if the baby was a boy he would not be pushed into football and he would decide for himself what he would do in life. Our little family was complete and I couldn't have been happier.

12

Samba Rhythms

In actual fact I had been away with England when I got a phone call to tell me Val had contracted the chicken pox. We had travelled to South America in the summer of 1977 for a close-season tour and were due to play Brazil, Argentina and Uruguay, which was fine except that our manager, Don Revie – in a move that rocked the football world – had decided to take up an offer to coach in the United Arab Emirates, leaving coaches Les Cocker and Bill Taylor in joint command of the squad. We lost 1–0 to Brazil in the Maracana stadium – I did not feature in the game – and a few of the lads went to see Ronnie Biggs afterwards, though I wasn't interested in meeting him. Then, after the game against Argentina, which we also lost, I found out about Val's chicken pox and asked Les and Bill if I could fly home early to be with Val. There was only the game against Uruguay still to be played, which I wasn't going to be picked for anyway, so my request was granted.

During the summer, City had signed England international Mick Channon for a club record £300,000 from Southampton as we looked to kick on from the previous season. With all the pieces in place for 1977/78, there was no reason why we shouldn't push Liverpool all the way again, but a failing over the years has been a propensity to shoot ourselves in the foot and what should have been a memorable campaign ended with just three wins in the last thirteen games after we had looked clear favourites to lift the title. We had the talent, but not the Liverpool winning mentality, and for the second successive year we lost our nerve in the home straight.

Looking at some of our results – a 6–2 win over Chelsea, a 3–1 win over Liverpool and a 4–1 win at Aston Villa – we certainly had enough quality, but what if we'd have really gone for it and splashed out on somebody like Trevor Francis? I reckon if we had invested in the right players it would have made all the difference. No disrespect to Mick Channon, but he was in his late twenties. Had Francis or Kenny Dalglish come to City instead of going to our rivals, who knows where it might have taken us. Maybe it was up to Tony Book to go in and demand money to take us to the next level; then again, maybe he was given a budget and had to work to it. Somebody should have had the balls to go for broke.

Colin Bell made his long-awaited comeback on Boxing Day 1977 and his return sparked an amazing run of seven consecutive league wins that put us top of the table with just a quarter of the campaign to go. Colin deserved the incredible reception he received when he ran out as a second-half substitute against Newcastle and the lift that gave every-one was incredible. But the lad was still struggling and it was only his sheer determination that had got him this far. I felt it was a sentimental decision to bring him back and that if he had been at any other club he would not have been selected. In today's game Colin would have taken a lot longer to return, if he ever had, but he was such a talisman for the club that no one would have denied him the right to try.

While Colin's comeback was a much-needed fillip, Dennis Tueart's move to New York Cosmos early in the New Year was a real setback. Dennis had been on the tour of South America with me during the pre-vious summer but he didn't play a great deal for England around that time. I sensed he had had his fill of the national team and resented being no more than a bit-part player. He was an ambitious lad and wanted to try pastures new. And who could blame him? The financial rewards in the North American Soccer League at that point were immense. Either that or Dennis had decided he didn't want any more disagreements with yours truly during five-a-side matches.

Ask any goalkeeper and they'll admit they love a game of five-a-side because it gives them the chance to strut their stuff and show they're not the big immobile lumps the outfield players would have you believe. There was an old bowling green at the back of Platt Lane on which we played our five-a-sides. I'd train with the team and then do my individual work with Bill Taylor before joining the lads to finish the morning off.

This particular day saw Dennis go in for a challenge on me and I reckoned the feisty little sod went over the top. I got up and proceeded to chase him around the pitch until I finally got hold of him, but before I could do anything he jumped up and butted me straight between the eyes. I put my hand up to my face and looked at it – it was covered in blood. I grabbed Dennis, intending to give him a taste of his own medicine, but Glyn Pardoe jumped on my back and we were both on top of poor Dennis who was being squashed beneath twenty-eight stones of footballer. I was close to Dennis's face by this point and it was only then that I realised the blood wasn't mine but his; he'd split his forehead open when he headed me and needed urgent treatment. We were both hauled in front of the gaffer and deservedly fined, but there were no hard feelings afterwards. It just showed the intensity with which we trained because we were so competitive and wanted to win things. It was soon forgotten, and, besides, ours was just one of the many ding-dongs that went on during training. Bill Taylor had instilled a will to win in us and sometimes it just boiled over, though nothing happened at Platt Lane that doesn't happen on a hundred other training pitches every week in England – and City of all clubs would be the first to admit that in light of recent events at Carrington involving Joey Barton and Ousmane Dabo. Besides, Tony gave me my fine back a few weeks later because he knew I hadn't instigated the incident, even though I'd been prepared to finish it.

In Europe, we ducked out at the first hurdle for the third time in five years, going out to Polish side Widzew Lodz on the away goals rule. We had led 2–0 at Maine Road at one point but conceded two late goals and their experience of playing in European competition year in, year out meant they just had the edge and they were content to play for a 0–0 draw on their own patch. Individually, we had plenty of internationalists who had played on the big stage many times before and it was frustrating that we weren't progressing to the latter stages of these competitions because we had enough talent to have won the UEFA Cup that year.

Our fourth-place finish in the league was also disappointing, though again, on a personal level, I felt my consistency levels had been high.

There was further proof that I'd gone from zero to hero with the City supporters, because they voted me player of the year for the second successive season. I'd now missed just one of the last 135 league games since my recall against QPR in 1975 meaning Keith MacRae had played reserve-team football for more than three years, which was tough on anybody, let alone a player who had arrived for a world-record fee.

Keith was a good lad and our relationship was competitive, but never less than friendly. He'd accepted the situation and one thing you find out about goalkeepers is that we realise if whoever is in the first team is performing well and doing his job, it's very difficult to break into the side because there is only one position to go for. When I was in the reserves, I was disappointed; not because Keith was doing well but because I wanted to play at the highest level and I'm sure Keith felt the same, though whether his ambition burned as brightly as mine, I don't know. He was a quiet bloke and if he had been thinking of moving on, he kept it to himself. At the start of a new season Booky had always told us we had to fight for our place, no matter whether we were a striker, defender or goalkeeper and that everyone had a chance. But, as I said, there was only one place up for grabs in our position so it was always going to be tougher. In addition, Alex Williams was starting to show promise in the youth team, and he had the makings of a very good keeper who would provide yet more competition for the number-one jersey in years to come. Along with youth-team coach Steve Fleet, the three of us trained together every day.

One of my proudest moments of 1978 was playing for England against Brazil at Wembley. It doesn't get much bigger than that and, this time, I played the full ninety minutes in front of our own fans. I'd been in many squads over the past couple of years and if Ray Clemence couldn't play, Peter Shilton would, although I think on this occasion a mixture of European club commitments and injury meant I was elevated from number three to number one. I always joined the squad knowing in the back of my mind I would be third in line, but preparing to play if needed. You had to be mentally ready if you were called upon and that's something I always prided myself on.

We walked out to a packed Wembley, our team containing the likes of Kevin Keegan and Trevor Brooking, the Brazilians with a team packed full of brilliant individuals such as Rivelino. I felt so proud to be representing my country on such a showpiece occasion. I had a few early touches of the ball but was beaten when Gil cut in from the right and hit a low drive with his left foot that beat me at my near post, which was disappointing. But while that dented my pride, I felt I made several fantastic saves after the break and the match ended honours even at 1–1.

Speaking to several people after the game, I learned that because of my height the Brazil players had practised firing free kicks and shots that would bounce just in front of me, in the belief that I would have difficulty getting down to deal with them. Two or three drives did skip up off the greasy Wembley surface and were difficult to deal with, but I felt pleased with myself. Val was watching from the stands, and after the match we celebrated into the night. I got blind drunk and fell asleep under the television in our hotel room.

I hoped that having proved myself under new manager Ron Greenwood I might get a run in the team, but for the next game I was back at number three yet again. When Greenwood took over, we had a meeting with him at Upton Park and he explained his vision for the future. He said he wanted to keep the basics of the squad together, but then turned to me and said that, unfortunately, he would only look to take two keepers rather than the current three. I had to get on with it and I thought that if there could only be two, I was going to do my damnedest to make sure I was one of them. As it happened, he always named three keepers in his squads, despite what he'd said.

The bonus of not playing regularly for the senior England team was that when there was an exotic tour in the offing with the England B team, my reward for being patient was to be the first choice for that particular trip. We played Malaysia, New Zealand and Singapore and it was a fantastic tour to take part in. While we didn't have a team packed with household names, each and every member of that squad wanted to play for England. Steve Daley, Peter Barnes, John Hollins, Gary Owen (my roommate), David Geddes and Paul Mariner were among the tour party and all of them were good, solid players who deserved international recognition of some kind. We flew out from Heathrow and landed in Kuala Lumpur for the first game of the tour and were invited by Guinness, who had a huge brewery, to enjoy their hospitality and a tour of the plant. They were keen for us to sample a new lager called Blondie, which we were of course happy to do and we were then given a fantastic lunch after being shown around by a guy who had sparred with Muhammad Ali prior to the legendary 'Rumble in the Jungle' fight. Then we faced the Malaysian national team. The game was played in Kuala Lumpur and it kicked off at midnight in front of a packed house of around 40,000, controlled by brutal security guards who operated a zero-tolerance policy with the locals and I believe there were huge numbers outside who couldn't get in.

The heat was intense and all the lads suffered from dehydration at some point – Steve Daley was sick during one game – and we drew 1–1, which I thought was a great result considering the conditions. Then we flew on to Australia, and on the journey I happened to pass our manager, Bobby Robson, who was writing notes on a clipboard. I couldn't help noticing that he'd written 'could have done better with the goal' next to my name. Malaysia's goal had been a real cracker that flew in the top corner, giving me no chance, and Bobby thought I could have done better! I'd have liked to have met the goalkeeper who could keep out shots like that because I would have been able to learn the art of being superhuman.

'What do you mean by that?' I asked, pointing at the offending entry. Bobby looked surprised and a little embarrassed by my question. 'I thought you were a little slow to react,' he replied. I told him that was his opinion, but as he was the boss and I respected him, there wasn't much more I could say. We stopped off in Sydney where I met up briefly with Ray Clemence, who was part of the Australian commentary team for the 1978 World Cup. We were given special dispensation to leave Sydney airport to have a look around the city before we caught our connecting flight to New Zealand. We had a meal on the coach, met Ray, had a quick tour around the city and then it was on with the journey and three more tough matches against New Zealand in Christchurch, Auckland and Wellington as well as another match against South Island in Dunedin. What a fantastic country it is, absolutely beautiful. I took part in my first real coaching sessions while we there, holding clinics for local kids, which I thoroughly enjoyed. To my surprise one of the brightest kids turned up at Maine Road some months later, having travelled halfway across the world, at his own expense, for a trial. Sadly things didn't work out for him, despite his commendable effort.

Because most of us had played for England several times on the tour – six matches in some cases – some of the lads who knew they'd never get a full cap wanted to know if they would get B-team caps. John Hollins and I were the senior members of the squad so we asked Jack Wiseman from the FA, who was on the tour with us, whether caps would be awarded, but he said they wouldn't. We suggested one cap for all the games and when we added that the lads were prepared to give up their win bonuses to help with the cost, Jack told us a cap would be awarded to each member of the squad. I always felt one of the best things about Ron Greenwood's era as England manager was the return of the England B games because it was a big stepping stone for a lot of players and a platform to show what they were capable of at international level. I think I ended up with a record number of ten caps at that level.

On our way home, we stopped off in Singapore for our final tour match, where another meal had been promised by the Guinness people. We had an official engagement with the high commissioner afterwards, but Bobby Robson said we could dine with the people from Guinness so long as we arrived on time for our evening event. After the lunch, a few lads wanted to go shopping and Bobby agreed, on the understanding that we returned to the hotel at five, giving us time to get changed for the high-commissioner visit.

After a quick hunt for souvenirs, we went back into the restaurant with the lads from Guinness and had a few more drinks. As the time moved towards five, John Hollins and I packed the other lads into taxis leaving just the two of us without transport. Because it was rush hour, there was no sign of a cab and both of us were the worse for wear after a few pints. It was our good fortune – or so I thought – that a rickshaw was passing, so we hailed it and told the driver to take us to the hotel. John got in and instantly fell asleep and when I got on board, the driver tried furiously to pedal, but just couldn't pull our combined weight. There was only one option. I took my jacket off, told the driver to get in the back and started pedalling. I was wearing my official England shirt and tie driving this bloody rickshaw through the streets of Singapore with Hollins fast asleep and a little Chinese guy sat with his feet up smoking a cigarette! You couldn't make it up. We eventually got back to the hotel but God only knows what people thought as they saw me riding past. I was thankful there weren't any England fans around. Not only that, I had to pay the so-called driver for the privilege. The coach had gone on without us so we dashed up to our rooms, got showered, changed and caught a cab – much to my relief – and got to our destination eventually.

It was while I was in Singapore that I learned of the gambling culture that existed in the Far East. We beat Singapore, the last opponents on the tour, easily, scoring eight without reply. Afterwards, I learned of a guy who had worked out that, because Singapore had beaten Malaysia recently and England had only drawn with them, Singapore should beat us. He bet his life savings on the result and we were told that, during the game, when it became obvious he would lose his bet, he jumped from the stadium roof, killing himself instantly. There had been some sort of a commotion as we played, but none of us knew why at the time.

13

An Opportunity Missed

After enjoying my best season with City during the 1977/78 campaign, in which we finished a respectable fourth in the league, we looked forward to continuing success. We'd established ourselves as one of the top clubs in the country along with Liverpool, Ipswich and Nottingham Forest – how times have changed – and all we needed to do was fine tune here and there. With Tony Book in the manager's office, and with Bill Taylor to help him on the training field, we had every reason to feel confident. But in a rash attempt to go that one step further, City, under the stewardship of chairman Peter Swales, took leave of its senses and made one of the worst decisions in the club's history. What followed was disastrous.

At least the club got one thing right that year: the signing of Kaziu Deyna in the summer of 1978. You couldn't argue with that decision. The first time I saw him in training I could tell he was a class act. He didn't seem to put much effort into anything, yet was a fantastic talent who probably arrived at the club two years too late. Had he arrived in 1976, he would have been a major star in England and would probably have helped us win the title, maybe even filling Colin Bell's boots. However, unbeknown to him, he couldn't have arrived at a worse time. He was a clinical finisher and a lovely man, whom I became friendly with during his time at Maine Road. One time, after an away match, we went for a drink in Fallowfield at a bar called The Sandpipers and after a couple of drinks, he asked if I could help him. I said I'd do whatever

I could and asked what was troubling him. 'I don't think my contract good,' he said in passable English. 'You help me, Joe?'

I pushed him to elaborate and he asked me what I was earning. I told him I didn't want to disclose that and he nodded, but said, 'I get £80 per week. Not enough, I think.' I nearly fell off my chair! It was very low, even for 1978. To put it in context I was on ten times his wages. He also said that his transfer fee had been paid in Rank Xerox copying machines and I couldn't help laughing at the thought. I felt so sorry for him and he deserved a lot more respect than he was getting from the club; after all he'd won more than one hundred caps for Poland and was a super-star in his homeland. I don't think he was ever destined to have a happy time in Manchester.

Other new lads who came in were the Futcher twins, Ron and Paul, plus Colin Viljoen. They were all decent players but not the calibre we needed to push on to the next level and this was perhaps the first sign that the club was not thinking for the future. A pre-season friendly in Holland should have given us a clue that this was going to be a tough year. Mike Doyle had moved on to Stoke by this time, bringing a seventeen-year career at Maine Road to an end, and, quite unintentionally, I'd had a hand in this. I'd lunged at a ball during a game and clashed with Mike's knee, causing an injury that kept him out of the team for several months. He lost his place and was transferred so I'd played a role in his departure. Now only Colin Bell had been at the club longer than me. We travelled to several countries, playing friendlies, and, six days before the new season was due to start, we faced AZ Alkmaar in a dress rehearsal for our opening league game against Norwich. It all went badly wrong as we were taken apart by Holland international Johnny Rep, losing 5–1. It wasn't the ideal preparation and we carried a hangover into our first four league games, drawing three and taking our customary thrashing from Liverpool at Maine Road, this time by four goals to one.

Despite all the things that would happen in the coming months, I still believe one of the biggest blows to the team that season was Kenny Clements breaking his leg against Ipswich in November. Kenny was a fantastic right-back: tall, good in the air, a fierce tackler and one of the most underrated players of that era; but that injury ended his career at Maine Road. There is a superstition in football that you never mess around with crutches, and a few weeks earlier, Kenny, a lovely kid who was as mad as a hatter, had been clowning around with a pair of crutches that happened to by lying around Platt Lane. A few of us told him it was bad luck and to put them down, but whether he believed us or not, the fact was he needed them for real after the Ipswich game.

Around that time, I got my first inkling that something big was happening behind the scenes at boardroom level. I'd been invited to a christening at the house of a friend of a director and as club captain, I was asked along as a sort of club representative. I didn't really know the guy and his wife that well, but out of courtesy Val and I agreed to go. As we were walking into the house, we were met by the host, Stan, and his wife. Val was ushered into the lounge, where there were a lot of guests, and I was shown into another room in which Peter Swales, Bill Adams and Ian Niven were ensconced. I thought it was all a bit cloak and dagger and after about a minute I realised that's exactly what it was.

'What do you think about Malcolm Allison coming back?' asked one of the directors – I can't recall who – and I was a little lost for words. We had Tony Book in charge and he was doing a great job – bear in mind by this point we were in the quarter-finals of both the League Cup and UEFA Cup – and a terrific coach in Bill Taylor. We were struggling to find our form in the league, but bringing Malcolm back smacked of desperation, when we weren't in a desperate situation. We'd lost Kenny Clements and were having a tough season, but the idea of Malcolm was, to me, ridiculous. With a bit more luck, we might have had successive league titles in 1977 and 1978. It was all wrong, but I could sense that it didn't really matter what I said. I could see it in their eyes; Malcolm was coming back and they were just gauging my reaction as a senior pro.

As the season approached halfway, it became difficult to keep pace with all the changes that were taking place but the sacking of Bill Taylor, shortly after that meeting, was devastating for the club and particularly for me, because I'd developed a very good relationship with him over the years. I felt he was cruelly forced out by board members, who were Malcolm-daft, and decisions were made behind Tony Book's back to accommodate that obsession. Bill was an excellent coach who was very influential on my playing career and I never forgot the things he taught me when I later moved into coaching myself. Sadly, he would die in tragic circumstances a few years later, suffering a brain haemorrhage when he still had so many years ahead of him in the game.

It was difficult to work out what Tony Book had done wrong. He had been appointed manager in 1974 and had steadied the ship after the turbulence created by Saunders, guiding the team to eighth place in his first full season in charge. We lifted the League Cup in 1976 and lost the title in 1976/77 by a single point to Liverpool, one of the greatest English club sides of all time. In 1977/78 – the season before Malcolm was brought back – we finished fourth equal and had a great run in the League Cup. But it wasn't just our results that were impressive: the team was playing very attractive, attacking football, which had led to higher attendances home and away. Indeed many good judges compared Tony's side favourably with the great City team of the late Sixties and early Seventies.

But to my mind, and despite these undoubted achievements, there were question marks about Tony's strength of character. After the League Cup win in 1976, not to mention the excellent campaigns in the first division, Tony was holding a winning hand. He should have gone to Swales and demanded money for quality players. If we had got a few more in I believe we could have put in a real challenge to Liverpool's dominance at the top of English football. Booky was very knowledgeable about the game and had done an excellent job in building up the squad, but, in my view, he wasn't determined enough to confront a man like Swales, a highly successful entrepreneur with a powerful personality. Once again it was an opportunity missed.

When Malcolm came back in January 1979 as first-team coach – or as some people described it, 'coaching overlord', whatever that meant – I was angry more than anything else. I wasn't happy with the underhand way things had been done and wasn't about to hide my feelings. It was a big gamble and I thought if he was going to come back at all, it should have been during the close season, not in the middle of it. What made things even worse was it soon became obvious that Malcolm's writ would run far beyond the training field. He would have the major say on the backroom staff, on transfers and on tactics, despite what was said for public consumption. He was the manager in everything but name and one of the saddest things was that as far as I could tell Tony seemed to accept his much-diminished role, despite his protestations to the contrary. Malcolm was such a powerful character, and Tony so quiet, that it was inevitable he would play second fiddle. It was awkward for everyone and you had to feel for Booky. I can't imagine it was a happy time for him and he certainly deserved more respect than he was shown by the club's hierarchy.

Ironically, despite the dip in our league form, we were doing well in Europe and had seen off FC Twente, Standard Liege and AC Milan prior to Malcolm's arrival, giving us a UEFA Cup quarter-final to look forward to in March. In between, Malcolm began his second coming and the team's decline continued. The FA Cup fourth-round tie at Shrewsbury Town was undoubtedly the low point of the season. It was the first time I'd been back to Gay Meadow since my loan spell there a decade before and not that much had changed. It was freezing, with the whole country in the grip of a cold snap, and we arrived the night before to stay in the Red Lion hotel, a short walk from the ground. A pitch inspection would be needed at ten the following morning so we arranged to walk to the ground for a bit of fresh air and arrived around nine. We stepped on to the pitch and even though the ground was solid and resembled an ice rink, we were told the inspection had already gone ahead and the match was on. There was no way that game should have been played and we felt we'd been stitched up, maybe because the *Match of the Day* cameras were there, but we had to go ahead with the game and the conditions would be the same for both teams. As it was, we were awful and there was no excuse for an embarrassing 2–0 defeat. They adapted quicker and deserved their win. Things weren't right at the club and it was hard to put a finger on exactly what it was.

A few days after the cup-tie Malcolm walked into the players' lounge and announced: 'I want you to speak to somebody because as a group of players, I think you could use some extra help.' We looked at each other, a little nonplussed, and wondered what he was up to this time. Then, a complete stranger walked in. Malcolm told us the guy was a psychologist and with that he upped and walked out, with no further explanation. We didn't know who this bloke was, or anything about his background, and after a few moments of him talking nonsense to us, Mick Channon got up and announced, 'I'm sorry, sir, but you're insulting my intelligence,' and left the room. I gave it a few more minutes before apologising and doing the same. The other senior pros soon followed suit because the idea was fundamentally flawed and Malcolm should have stayed to field any criticism; the end result, a walk out by the players, was highly embarrassing for all concerned.

England had plenty of matches during this campaign and I felt more than a little frustrated that, despite my patience and consistency over the past three years, I still wasn't being rewarded with a run of games in the national side. What exactly did I have to do to impress Ron Greenwood? If Ray Clemence and Peter Shilton had an edge on me in previous seasons – in the eyes of the England manager at least – I was sure that I now had one on them. At worst I was on a level playing field but there was still no reward as Greenwood opted for the safe interchange of Shilts and Clem for the top spot, while I remained at number three. I was at the top of my game and desperate for my chance. I'd never let England down when I had played, but I was being thrown scraps to keep me from biting; the odd friendly here, a B international there.

I never thought the rotation system was fair because they only rotated it between two and not three. My view was that we should have stuck with one keeper and if you came in and did well, you should have kept your place. According to people like Bill Shankly, I was the best in the country at that time so I'd be lying if I said it didn't rankle with me. But it's always been a game of opinions and Ron Greenwood's just happened to be that I was third in the pecking order.

I was included in virtually every England squad from 1976 to 1982 – probably thirty to forty times – so it's not hard to imagine why I was so frustrated at being able to count my cap haul on two hands. I played under just two England managers, Don Revie and Ron Greenwood. Revie was articulate, demanding of players and very autocratic; everything was run according to his vision for the national side, which of course is the way it should be. He kept a dossier on every player we were playing against and you'd get the information whether you were in the team or not. Yet his way was more suited to club management because his regime was too rigid. I have enormous respect for what he achieved – nobody can take that away from him and he was also a legend as a Manchester City player. Greenwood was completely the opposite: a great coach – one of the best I've worked with – but not the greatest man manager. He knew his stuff and was meticulous in his analysis of the game and of the opposition; he also has to be given credit for encouraging freedom of expression in his teams. For me, his biggest flaw was that he was easily influenced by the London press and I think that had a bearing on my involvement with the England side.

I remember that before a game against Brazil, Greenwood said, 'Every time I watch you play club football, I keep hearing the fans chanting "England, England's No.1" – you're playing against Brazil now, so go out and show me you are.' I felt he was giving me my chance to prove him wrong and I had a good game that night, but it didn't change anything and I was soon the odd one in three again, which disappointed me.

Back at City, we went out of Europe in March against eventual winners Borussia Moenchengladbach, effectively ending our season, and we finished fifteenth in the league. During the close season, I was invited to America to take part in a coaching clinic with *Football Focus* anchorman and former Arsenal legend Bob Wilson at Tampa Bay Rowdies. I'd been recommended by former referee Gordon Hill, who was doing a bit of consultancy in the States, where the NASL was still hugely popular. We coached at South Florida University and it was fantastic – a wonderful experience – and Val and the kids came along, too. Steve Coppell and Paul Barron were staying at the same hotel, the Bay Harbour Inn, as was comedian Jasper Carrot and his entire film crew, who were making a documentary on American soccer. In fact, he'd arranged the Tampa Bay Rowdies cheerleaders to strut their stuff on the beach by our hotel. Their name? The Fannies . . . only in America! The opening credits for the programme featured a mechanical, swimming Donald Duck circling around the pool – that was my lad Andrew's and he enjoyed telling his pals that his favourite toy was a television star. The coaching clinics were no more than babysitting sessions. The stuff we were trying to teach the kids – of all shapes and sizes – was so far advanced to anything they had previously experienced as to be ineffective. It would have been far more beneficial to American soccer if Bob and I had been asked over to coach their coaches, so that when we returned home, they could carry on where we'd left off. Nevertheless I enjoyed the experience and it was a nice break in the sun for the family as well.

On one occasion I met Southampton manager Lawrie McMenemy around the pool at our hotel and got chatting. As we discussed various aspects of coaching and the state of the game back home, a waiter came out and said to Lawrie that he had a phone call from England. He thought it was club business so opted to take the call privately in the lobby. He came back about ten minutes later, absolutely fuming. 'I can't bloody believe it!' he said as he climbed back on to his sun lounger. He looked at me and said, 'I cannot believe your manager. He has only gone and spent £750,000 on a striker from Preston.' We asked who it was and he replied: 'Michael Robinson'. The general reaction was, 'who?' I asked why he was annoyed and he explained that, in his opinion, Robinson – a young player with little in the way of a track record – was probably worth less than half that amount. From now on every lower-league club would be looking for that kind of money. In Lawrie's view Malcolm Allison had just made his, and the lives of twenty other first-division managers, a lot harder.

Then Lawrie added, 'And I've asked if I could buy you for a fair price and have been told no by City.'

'Can you repeat that?' I asked, incredulously.

It was the first I'd heard of it. He explained he had made a bid for me but the club had turned it down. It was around the time of the fire-damaged, stock-clearance sale that had already seen Big Mal sell Dave Watson, Asa Hartford, Gary Owen, Brian Kidd and Peter Barnes. Therefore, it didn't take a genius to work out that I, being one of the few remaining senior pros, must have looked a likely bet to follow the others out of the door. Mal was clearing out anybody that he believed would disagree with his methods and replacing them with kids and lower-league players who would be glad of an opportunity to play for a big club. It was confirmed later by Peter Swales that the offer had been made but the club would never sell me. He said whatever happened in the coming months and years, I'd be there and that he wasn't going to sell his best players. I felt the horse had bolted somewhat in that regard, but he just said, 'You've got a job for life here, Joe.' That statement would prove to be not entirely true.

I met up with Rodney Marsh for the first time since he left Maine Road in 1976 during my stay in Tampa and we got on fine. I watched him play for the Rowdies – strictly exhibition stuff – with the Fannies jumping around in the background and a cannon going off every time there was a shot on goal. It suited Marshy down to the ground. The one thing I remember was the way the Tampa fans made a day of it, arriving early, eating as families, enjoying the entertainment on offer inside and outside the stadium and lapping up the sunshine. Despite a crowd of more than 40,000 we got away quickly after the game, unlike the hour or so it took to get a mile from Maine Road. Bob Wilson was with Marshy and me and we went for a drink in a bar called the Brass Balloon and talked about his troubled last year at Maine Road. He said he still couldn't believe he hadn't had the backing of the other players during his dispute with Booky and I explained that most of us didn't want to become embroiled in disputes between players and managers. He wouldn't accept that, maintaining we'd been in the wrong, but we enjoyed the evening and parted on good terms.

When I got back to City for pre-season training in July 1979 it was announced that Malcolm had been appointed manager, with Tony moved upstairs as general manager, not that it would make any difference to the balance of power within Maine Road, as Malcolm had been in complete control since returning eight months before. Prior the campaign, he asked me if I'd take on the captaincy of the side. Although I would have been honoured to accept, I felt it was wrong for a keeper to take on that job because free kicks and suchlike frequently needed to be organised at the other end of the pitch. What use was I sixty yards away? However, I was more than happy to become club captain, leading to a wider role off the pitch. The armband was handed instead to Paul Power, an excellent choice.

But despite being given this great honour I was deeply unhappy with Malcolm's stewardship of the club. His big idea when he came back to Maine Road was to replace what he saw as ageing stars with younger players, who were better able to cope with the power running he thought essential in the modern game. To build up their strength Malcolm put the emphasis in training on developing their body strength through power weights and other similar techniques. That is fair enough but players need more than just strength and pace: they also need technique, touch and experience at the highest level, qualities that the new boys patently did not have. He had replaced seasoned internationals with the likes of Bobby Shinton, Barry Silkman, Paul Sugrue, Dragoslav Stepanovic and Stuart Lee. Gary Owen had been shipped out to West Brom with Peter Barnes, and Gary's dad told me that he'd driven him to the Hawthorns in floods of tears because he never wanted to leave City. The walls were crumbling around us, the transfer policy was suicidal and if the emperor didn't have any clothes, nobody had the bottle to tell him. At least, not yet.

14

War with Malcolm

Steve Daley became a British record signing when Malcolm paid £1.4 million for his services in 1979. I knew Steve from the time we'd been on tour with the England B squad. He was a hard-working player, but even he realised that the club had paid well over the odds for him and whatever transfer funds had been available must have been dwindling pretty quickly. On the back of the nightmarish 78/79 campaign, the 1979/80 season was also a miserable affair in which things went from bad to worse. Somehow, we managed back-to-back victories on five separate occasions, which I think kept Malcolm and Tony in a job. Malcolm tried everything to rediscover the magic touch, but the harder he tried, the worse things got. He even brought in rugby coaches to take training sessions, but the revolutionary ideas of his heyday were no longer working, and, crucially, the players weren't a patch on the squad he had to work with in the Sixties. The squad he'd inherited was ripe and ready and just needed a jump start, but he chose to decimate the team and rebuild, so he only had himself to blame.

Things were also going from bad to worse for Kaziu Deyna. We flew out to Poland to play a friendly with his old club Legia Warsaw – part of the transfer deal – and there were 100,000 fanatical Poles inside Legia's stadium. Kaziu's young son and pregnant wife were also invited over for the game and afterwards there was a reception and a meal. The Legia players sat on one side of the table and we sat on the other with representatives from the Polish Army at the top of the table, along with our directors. There wasn't any camaraderie between the teams so I asked the waiter if we could buy the Legia players a drink. The waiter looked a little concerned so I asked Bernard Halford to make the request to the powers-that-be; they agreed to one drink, which the Legia players seemed greatly to appreciate, resulting in a much friendlier atmosphere.

Unfortunately, it wasn't long after we heard that Kaziu's wife had been rushed to hospital where she would need to spend the remaining six months of her pregnancy, meaning he would have to bring up his young son alone in Manchester, further compounding his already numerous difficulties in England. I knew he had a problem with drink in the weeks and months after, but, with all the pressures in his life, it was hardly surprising. He was a very funny man, with a much better command of English than he let on and when it came to the running sessions around Wythenshawe Park that Malcolm had reintroduced, Kaziu would turn up in the morning and simply tell the physio, 'Hamstrung. Very bad.' His numerous niggles and knocks, I'm certain, were concocted to avoid training, but then he wouldn't be the first or the last to pull a stroke like that. The simple truth was that he was desperately unhappy at being separated from his loved ones and it was sad to see such a fine player, and man, go downhill so rapidly.

I was happy with my own form and started the season well, with one of my best performances coming in a League Cup tie away to Sheffield Wednesday, which was amazing considering the chance I'd taken. Val and I had been around to some friends the evening before. It was the first time I had had a few drinks on the night before a game, yet I was outstanding for the entire ninety minutes. We drew 1–1 and, in the second leg, played well again but fell behind to a penalty. That was despite me saving the first effort and then seeing the referee order it to be retaken. Fortunately, Tony Henry scored twice in the last two minutes to send us through to the next round.

This was also the season Granada began filming a season-long documentary called *City!* and the fallout from certain parts of that film brought things to an explosive head between Malcolm and me. We'd just been beaten 4–0 at home by Liverpool (again) and the film crew went into the inner sanctum of the boardroom where Malcolm began openly to criticise me. Kenny Dalglish had scored two goals that afternoon and turned our defence, particularly young Tommy Caton, inside out. The crew finished their filming in the boardroom and the presenter sought me out in the dressing room, where I'd been having a shower. We knew they'd been granted access all areas and we accepted they would be in our faces, but when they asked me what I thought of Malcolm's statement that one of the Liverpool goals had been down to me I asked exactly what had been said. I was told that Malcolm had said, in response to someone saying Dalglish had scored a great second goal: 'Great goal? It bounced five times in front of Joe before he moved.' I wasn't happy, to say the least. While he was entitled to his opinion, and maybe I was at fault, he should have been saying it to me first, not to a camera crew eager for controversy.

This was also my testimonial year and I was grateful to the chairman for the offer. The opposition for the game was decided by Mr Swales, who reckoned it would be a good idea to fulfil a promise to play Dave Watson's new team Werder Bremen. I thought about it and agreed it was a good idea because Big Dave had been a hugely popular figure during his years at Maine Road. Testimonials invariably involved the same type of opponents – Manchester United or a combined Merseyside XI – and I thought something different might work to my advantage. There had never been European opposition before for one of these games and I thought it might capture the supporters' imagination. It was arranged with the help of Tudor Thomas and the chairman assured me all expenses would be covered by the club. The problem was that Dave Watson left Bremen for Southampton shortly before the game was due to be played and there was no way out of the commitment we'd made. It was a disaster.

Even the weather conspired against me that evening, with torrential rain further hampering the attendance, which was poor to say the least. I ran down the tunnel and could see the Kippax was reasonably full, but as I ran onto the pitch, I noticed that the other three stands were virtually empty. Harry Godwin, the man who discovered me, made a presentation before kick-off but I'd be lying if I didn't admit I was bitterly disappointed with the turnout, which was less than 9,000. I respected the fact that it was up to the fans if they wanted to attend – it was their choice – and it was another admission price on top of their match-day costs. Nevertheless, I had hoped for a few more and the club and police had been expecting closer to 15,000. I think my game and Tommy Booth's were the death knell for testimonials, which just weren't being supported any more and

I think only Paul Lake has had one in the last twenty-five years. I do have to thank Tudor Thomas, a dear friend, and his committee, who worked incredibly hard to put the game on. I will always be grateful for their efforts.

It did make me wonder what it was all about. I'd been with the club since I was sixteen and I'd looked forward to the evening because so many people close to me had worked hard to make it a success. I was very grateful to the people who did attend, because they were magnificent. The papers were scathing in their condemnation of the City fans that hadn't bothered to turn up, asking why they hadn't taken the chance to turn out and show their appreciation of my efforts over the years. If I'm honest, it left a bit of a sour taste, especially when we beat Manchester United 2–0 at Maine Road a few days later. With more than 50,000 fans in the ground, it was embarrassing to hear the United fans sing, 'Corrigan, Corrigan where's your fans?' Alex Stepney had recently had his testimonial, which attracted 35,000 people. I accepted what had happened and just got on with it, but the size of the crowd made me wonder about moving on. But, of course, the club was in my blood and I had to put it behind me. Besides, there was enough happening at Maine Road to take my mind off such disappointments. Today, of course, most top players are so rich it doesn't matter whether they have a testimonial or not, and several who have been honoured in this way have ended up donating some or all of the proceeds to charity, which is better still.

We ended 1979 as miserably as we would begin 1980. Malcolm's golden touch had disappeared and in a desperate attempt to revive our fortunes his tactics frequently bordered on the bizarre. During our game away to Brighton on 29 December, we played without any forwards, because, he told us, it was muddy down the middle of the pitch. It was neither innovative nor fresh; it was just plain daft. His idea was to use wingers on the grassy flanks instead, but, by half time, we were 4–0 down. We had to change the formation ourselves and went back to 4–4–2, but it was embarrassing that Tommy Booth and I were the ones to instigate it and not Malcolm. It was further proof of his growing eccentricity.

At least we'd drawn fourth-division strugglers Halifax Town in the FA Cup and could begin the New Year with a confidence-boosting victory, or so we thought. It turned out that we would leave The Shay at rock bottom following one of the biggest cup shocks of all time. We hadn't played well and were lucky to lose only 1–0 and it epitomised just how bad things had become under Malcolm. After the game I was walking out of the stadium behind Steve Daley, who was getting dog's abuse from the City fans. It was so bad that he snapped and grabbed one by the throat. Fortunately, I was on hand to pull him away; God only knows what might have happened otherwise. Yes it was romantic for neutrals, and a perfect example of the so-called magic of the FA Cup, but it doesn't feel romantic and there's a distinct lack of magic when you're on the end of a giant-killing act. NASA had spent £10 million getting a man to the moon, while Malcolm had spent £6 million but couldn't get past Halifax; the jokes came thick and fast. There was no light at the end of our tunnel and the team's reaction to the Halifax debacle was to fail to register a single win in seventeen league games, which tells its own story about our morale. But for Dennis Tueart's return, we would have gone down. As it was, Dennis's five goals in the last eleven games saved us, and just one defeat in the last eight matches, rescued our sorry campaign when it was dying on its knees.

The old maxim that you never go back in football had been proved true in Malcolm's case, but certainly hadn't held true with Tueart and it was good to see him back and at his best. We finished seventeenth, our worst season in thirteen years. All the players Malcolm had signed for over-inflated fees – Steve Daley and Michael Robinson included – couldn't cope with the weight of expectation and visibly wilted under the strain. Everything Malcolm had done during his second spell was going wrong and if something wasn't done, we'd be in real danger of being relegated next time around. As club captain, I was attending supporters events, but couldn't say what I really felt or tell the fans what was happening behind the scenes because it would been wrong. On a personal note, I was proud to accept my third player-of-the-year award from the City fans and I'm told only Richard Dunne with four awards can better this.

I added a few more England caps during the summer against Australia, Wales and Northern Ireland and it gave me a chance to throw off the shackles of club football. I enjoyed the summer break as best as I could, but wondered what the coming season held for us considering we had no money and no prospect of new blood for the 1980/81 season. Despite the doom and gloom, we travelled to Portugal for a pre-season tour and thoroughly enjoyed the trip; we remained unbeaten after drawing 0–0 with Porto and beating Sporting Lisbon 2–1 in the Stadium of Light. With victories over Braga and Breda, we returned home full of optimism for the upcoming campaign, but it was a false dawn.

The 1980/81 season began disastrously with no sniff of a win and I'd had enough. As club captain I was under increasing pressure from the other lads to speak up, so I did. The players held a meeting to express their concern and it was clear that nobody was happy. It was down to me to stand up and air the grievances of my teammates and I did exactly that to Malcolm in front of the lads after we had lost miserably again. I told him how it was and that his way wasn't working, but after I'd finished, I looked around the dressing room and nobody looked me in the eye. Nobody had the bottle to back me up and I was left looking like the bad guy in Malcolm's eyes. But I was prepared to stick to my guns because Malcolm was destroying the club. Something needed to be said, and I'd said it.

When nothing changed I lost patience and said publicly that the majority of players in the squad weren't good enough. I didn't mean that as a personal dig at individuals, but what was being asked of them wasn't fair and they weren't able to cope with such intense pressure. Many were too young and too inexperienced and it showed. Whatever momentum we'd picked up in Portugal was soon forgotten and we were back to having rugby coaches in or whatever harebrained scheme was cooked up next, putting us back to square one.

On the bus home after yet another morale-crushing loss, I mentioned to Piccadilly Radio's resident City commentator Brian Clarke that something needed to be said in public about what was happening at the club. Clarkey said, 'OK, let's start the tape and do an interview.' And we did. I said everything I thought needed saying and that was the end of the matter. I felt a load had been lifted. There were no scathing attacks or character assassinations; it was simply my opinion on an unsustainable situation. The management structure was totally wrong; Tony was general manager and Malcolm was team manager, yet Malcolm was calling the shots. In particular, I couldn't forget what happened after our defeat to Borussia Moenchengladbach in the UEFA quarter-final: Mal appeared on the coach in his sheepskin, fedora and tracksuit bottoms, while outside Tony was pushing a big skip containing our kit across the concourse. It was embarrassing and had gone on for much too long. My interview with

Brian Clarke was aired the following day and then picked up by the national media. Whether I was right to do it or not, it was too late and, after it had been broadcast, there was no turning back. Maybe I shouldn't have criticised my teammates, but things had come to a head and I felt it had to be done. If nothing else, maybe it would shake the club out of its complacency.

It went out over the August bank-holiday weekend and, on the Monday morning, the day before we were due to play Stoke in the League Cup, Malcolm called me in to his office at Maine Road. He said that I was totally out of order, he wasn't having it and that I lacked respect for my teammates, for him and for the club. I denied that and said I just felt I needed to speak up as the senior pro. If I'd been disrespectful, it hadn't been my intention. It didn't seem to matter because he suspended me for two weeks and fined me two weeks' wages. By coincidence, Val had arranged to take the kids away with her mum for a caravan holiday in North Wales. She was due to go the following day and I was helping her pack when Peter Swales phoned to tell me he wanted a meeting with Malcolm and I in his offices in Altrincham.

I arrived to find Malcolm and Tony Book already there and Peter said that he wanted me to put an apology out in the local press. I asked what I had to apologise about – I'd spoken from the heart but he said things had to be done the right way. He placed a piece of paper with a prepared statement on it and asked: 'Do you agree with it?' 'No,' I said. 'I don't agree with it at all, but if this is the way you want to go, I'll do it.'

To keep the peace, I went along with it but the next day, Swales called me and asked if I'd meet him in Altrincham again. I still had time to help Val pack up the car, and, as we did, I noticed someone lurking at the end of our drive. Val reckoned he was holding something so I went down to take a closer look and it turned out to be a photographer from the *Manchester Evening News*. He'd been taking shots of me putting cases in the car and I asked why. He told me that the sports editor had instructed him to get pictures because Val was leaving me in view of what had happened the day before. He added, 'Now I've got proof.' I put him right in no uncertain terms and told him that if any of the pictures appeared in the paper, I'd sue.

As it turned out none were published, but it made me realise how football was changing, and not for the better. With Val and the kids safely on their way to Wales, I travelled the short distance to the chairman's offices and wondered what was in store this time. It was just the two of us on this occasion and he said: 'Listen, I understand what's going on but I think you were wrong in what you did, but I'm not going to endorse a two-week fine.' It was just as well, because I'd spoken to Gordon Taylor at the PFA just an hour before and he said there was no way the club could dock me a fortnight's pay. I told Swales as much and said I could be suspended or fined, but not both. He replied that he had told Malcolm that there would be no suspension because he wanted his best players playing, not sitting in the stands, so apparently the suspension was lifted.

'If that's your decision, then fine,' I said. 'So long as I can play, I don't mind.'

I went home and later that evening Harry Gregg called me to chat about the past twenty-four hours. I explained the situation and he told me he understood why I'd done what I'd done but then added, 'Whatever you do, don't play at Stoke tomorrow.' I told him that I was paid to play and that was what I would do but he insisted. 'Joe, in my experience both as a player and a manager, don't play tomorrow because you'll either get badly injured or you'll make a howler.'

I appreciated his concern, but I was paid to play for Manchester City and if they needed me I'd be there. Incredibly, Harry's prophecy came true and within the first half hour I went out to block a one-on-one with a Stoke forward and we clattered into each other, both of us sustaining nasty knocks. My knee swelled up like a balloon, though I managed to make it to half-time; the other lad was taken off on a stretcher with a cracked kneecap that he later had to have pinned. Tommy Booth went in goal after the break and we managed a 1–1 draw, but I was ruled out for a fortnight. Harry still reminds me to this day that I should have listened to him. That injury brought to an end 195 consecutive league appearances and gave long-suffering Keith MacRae some first-team action. He played four times before I was passed fit, and those would be his last appearances in the senior side before his move to Portland Timbers later that season.

There were a couple of bizarre incidents in the wake of that injury, incidents that still make me laugh today even if they weren't so funny at the time. The first came after I had just had an air splint (something like a balloon) put on my injured knee by Dr Norman Luft. Because Val was away, and I needed help to move around, Dr Luft and his wife, Jackie, very kindly offered to put me up at their house for a short time. One night, after we had enjoyed a few drinks, they carried me up to bed. Unfortunately, the valve on the air splint came out and it promptly deflated. I called for help and Jackie came into my bedroom. Seeing what had happened she bent over my knee and started to blow the splint up. But just at that moment Norman came into the room, clutching a bottle of brandy. He must have seen Jackie with her head over my leg, puffing and panting, and wondered what on earth his wife was up to. Of course it was all totally innocent, despite how it looked.

The second happened four days later, after I was back at home in our house in Sale. I had been out and had just unlocked the front door and gone inside when I tripped and fell flat on my face. I couldn't move and would probably have been lying there for hours if our alarm system hadn't been connected to the police station. The police responded to the alarm and I was relieved when two burly cops appeared in our hall and proceeded to rescue me.

I returned in time for the Manchester derby at Old Trafford but something didn't feel right that day; at the time, I couldn't put my finger on it. We arrived at the ground suited up, as usual, but Malcolm arrived wearing a tracksuit, something I'd never seen him do on a match day. In the changing rooms, his suit was hung up in a clear-plastic-dry-cleaning bag. It seemed a little odd and later on, we discovered he'd been having problems at home so, along with the team's misfortunes, he was having a rough time of it and the pressure must have been immense. From the first time I played against Manchester United I had a 'delightful' rapport with their supporters. They used to call me Frankenstein, or similar, and the good thing about their insults was that it geed me up even more. Every good result against the Reds – and I was involved in a lot of victories over them – was extra sweet. At least we produced a battling display on the pitch, scoring a last-minute equaliser to secure a 2–2 draw. It was a fantastic feeling being in front of 12,000 City fans going bananas and I got carried along by the euphoria. As we left the pitch, Ray Wilkins came up and said, 'Christ, you kept them in the game today. I can't believe you've been out injured and came back today and played like that.'

For Malcolm, his time at Maine Road was almost up. In October 1980, following defeats at home to Liverpool and away to Leeds, both he and Tony were sacked. I learned what had happened through the press and we were never told officially by the club. Ken Barnes became caretaker manager but, at the next training session after the sackings, Malcolm turned up at Platt Lane with his usual press entourage. I used to train at the back of Platt Lane and didn't know that much about it, although I saw him gather the team together to tell them that he was leaving. I thought it was wrong of Malcolm to turn up unannounced but that was the way he was. Instead of walking away with dignity, he wanted to be larger than life and create a lot of fuss. If he'd wanted to say good-bye, it should have been done privately. But that was Malcolm Allison and you either loved him or hated him for it. Ken asked me to trot over for a moment and I went and shook Malcolm's hand and then got on with what I'd been doing. We had an important game to play at the weekend and needed to focus on that, not on Malcolm and his sideshow.

The second coming of Malcolm Allison had been nothing short of a disaster. Before he arrived City were on the verge of greatness and who knows what could have been achieved. After eighteen months with him in charge the club was in crisis. In fact the decision to reappoint him may well have been the worst in City's long and proud history. They say that failure is an orphan while success has many fathers. That is certainly true in this case. In the 1990s Peter Swales conceded that the decision to bring Malcolm in was his biggest mistake but that he 'got talked into it' by others on the board.

15

The Name's Bond...

It wasn't long before Peter Swales found a new manager following the sackings of Malcolm and Tony. I wasn't in the country when it was announced who was coming in but whoever it was they had a hell of a job ahead of them. On 11 October 1980 we'd lost 3–1 at West Brom under Ken Barnes; it was our eleventh game of the season without a win. After that game, I travelled to Bucharest with England for a vital World Cup qualifier that was due to be played four days later. I didn't play in the game, which ended 2–1 to Romania, and, while I was away, John Bond had been installed as City's new manager. I first met him on the Friday morning after returning from international duty. He seemed enthusiastic, and, more importantly from my point of view, he said what I wanted to hear. 'We're doing everything from scratch from now on, Joe. I'm going to bring a few new players in and you're going to be a big part of the future, but I know there are one or two things that need sorting.'

One or two things was an understatement, but I said I was there for him and would back him all the way. He was no idiot and was well aware of the problems the club had experienced over the previous few months. His first question to me was about the situation with Malcolm that had resulted in a fine. I explained that I felt it was my job to speak out about what was happening to the club I loved.

'Fine,' he said, 'I've no problem with that. Let's just go on from here.' And we did. He brought John Benson and John Sainty in as coaches and signed Gerry Gow from Bristol City for £175,000 and Tommy Hutchison and Bobby McDonald from Coventry City for bargain fees; it was fantastic business and it proved to me that Bond was the right man for the job. He knew the youngsters were under pressure and had brought in seasoned professionals to take some of the weight off their shoulders. It was simple yet inspired.

Bond was a graduate of the West Ham football academy and he wanted to play attractive, attacking football, which is also what the City fans craved. His coaches had worked with him at Norwich and formed a tight unit, with John Sainty among the best I ever worked with. Bond was very forthright in his views, but he was definitely a player's manager. He was a good coach, too, and I was looking forward to being part of his vision for Manchester City. Bond left Ken Barnes in charge of the team for the Birmingham City match – the first game since he'd arrived – and told us he wasn't going to interfere, choosing to watch from the main stand. We lost 1–0 to a last-minute Archie Gemmill penalty and Bond came down after the match and said, 'I've seen what I wanted to see and I know what we need to do. There's a lot of work ahead. Get changed and we'll get cracking on Monday morning.'

He gave us an instant lift and we won our next four games on the bounce, including a victory that put us into the quarter-final of the League Cup. He worked quickly and efficiently to boost the squad and I couldn't help but be impressed by the players he brought in. I'd known Tommy Hutchison for donkey's years and he was a quality player who just oozed class. I didn't know Bobby McDonald, a marauding full-back, that well, though Gerry Gow was a well-respected midfielder and someone we'd eventually nickname Cappa de Monte Ankles on account of his fragility in that particular area of his body. Gerry was a gritty Glaswegian who, despite his slight frame, was as hard as nails. He'd always been a tough opponent whenever we'd played Bristol City and he was exactly what we needed – a wily old dog to prowl the midfield and one that wasn't afraid to bite. He was a great asset to our side – they all were – and a much-underrated player, and he added steel to the midfield.

Bond knew how to use the width of Maine Road to maximum effect and would employ Hutch to hug the flanks as he'd done at his previous clubs. In addition Bobby Mac's cavalier gallops forward added an element of surprise to our attacks, giving the side a new dimension. Mentally, we were a new team. There were no strangers coming in to take specialist training sessions, there were no women taking stretching classes, no hypnotists, psychologists or wizards with magic potions – just our own coaches concentrating on football, fitness and tactics. It was all about getting the ball out wide, getting crosses into the near post for our strikers and both Kevin Reeves and Dennis Tueart thrived on the service.

We were on a roll and whether you're on winning or losing runs, it's difficult to get out of the habit. We won eight of Bond's first ten games in charge, and, despite his new signings being cup-tied for the League Cup, the young lads that came into replace them carried on the good work because we were playing to a plan that actually worked. It was simple; we went out on match days and did what we did on the training pitch, where, incidentally, the emphasis was always on playing football. We played within our limits, but performed to our strengths and it was a great time to be a City fan and a City player. We were pulling clear of the bottom three and winning games that we'd have got nothing from prior to Bond's arrival. One game, at Goodison, saw us slugging it out with Everton and, as a cross came in to our box, I had to dive at the feet of one of their players. Tommy Caton, who got entangled in the challenge, gave me a clout with his boot, but I thought no more about it, got up and carried on. It had been an atrocious day and I had constantly been wiping the rain and mud out of my eyes. I was wearing a pair of green Peter Bonetti goalkeeping gloves and each time I wiped away the rain, they became browner and browner until I realised it wasn't mud or rain I was wiping away, but blood. Tommy's studs had gashed the top of my head and Roy Bailey ran on to see if he could patch me up until half-time, which he did by liberally applying Vaseline to the wound.

Our club doctor wasn't there that day for some reason, so, at the break I had to go into Everton's changing room to be treated by their doctor. As I walked in, I noticed a few of their players sniggering. I wasn't sure why and sat on the treatment table while their club doctor began applying stitches. After a few moments he winced in pain and I could feel a tugging on top of my head – he'd stitched his hand to my head! He eventually freed himself and I went out to play a part in a 2–0 win. Later, I went for a drink in the players' lounge and got talking with a few Everton players, who explained why they'd been laughing. They told me I'd been taking a chance being treated by the doctor, or Mr

Magoo as he was affectionately known, who had a reputation for the odd faux pas.

By the time of the FA Cup third round, we'd won eleven of Bond's first fifteen games. As the draw was being made, I felt it was inevitable that we would draw Malcolm Allison's new club, Crystal Palace. Don't ask me why, but I just knew we'd get them. The question most people were asking was: how would the players Malcolm had blooded react? Tommy Caton, Ray Ranson, Nicky Reid and Steve Mackenzie, all twenty or under, owed a debt of gratitude to Malcolm; rewind a dozen or so years, and you could throw my name into the mix too. We had no axe to grind, no grudge to bear; we were totally focused on winning and not distracted by the media circus that rolled into town with Malcolm. It showed in our performance; we won comfortably, by four goals to nil. The filming of the *City* documentary was almost over, and I later remember seeing footage of Malcolm during the half-time interval asking his lads to give him one free kick, one chance, anything to get back in the game. He'd run out of ideas and in many ways it was a real shame, because, in his heyday, he was up there with the greatest coaches in the world.

The games were coming thick and fast and but for referee Alf Grey we might even have laid the Liverpool bogey. We'd drawn the toughest of the three teams left in the competition and we would play the League Cup semi-final first leg at Maine Road. We thought we'd gone 1–0 up when Kevin Reeves headed home a perfectly good goal, but Grey, inexplicably, disallowed it. Reeves was certainly not offside, and hadn't fouled anyone, so only the ref knew the reason he'd robbed us of a lead. Typically perhaps, Liverpool then went up the other end and Ray Kennedy scored the only goal of the game. Our disappointment at not beating them showed just how far we'd come in the space of a few months.

Then it was back to the FA Cup and another pairing tinged with irony. We drew Bond's old side Norwich and again we cruised home, winning 6–0 following a phenomenal performance. We were on fire to such an extent that we felt we could still turn around a 1–0 deficit in the semi-final, second leg at Anfield. We almost did, outplaying Liverpool and drawing 1–1, with young Dave Bennett's header crashing against the bar in the last minute; what a famous win that would have been. We were both elated and devastated at the way things had gone, and, but for a coat of paint, we might have been going back to Wembley for the first time since 1976. I got showered and dressed and then went straight onto the coach after the game. While I was waiting for the other lads, with my head pressed against the window, I saw Bill Shankly passing. He spotted me, gave a wry smile and came onto the coach and sat down next to me. You couldn't help but be in total awe of the man and we chatted for a few moments about the game and how unfortunate we'd been. As he got up to go, he said, 'What you've got to remember now, son, is that you're the best goalkeeper in the country – by far – just keep on going the way you are and you'll be all right.' With that, he got off the coach. I never saw him again and he died not long after. Those words would stay with me and I understood why he got the very best from his players. What a wonderful, charismatic man whose passing was a terrible loss to football.

We still had Wembley in our sights as we prepared to take on fourth division Peterborough United at London Road for a place in the last eight of the FA Cup. John Bond was ill and didn't travel so John Benson and John Sainty took over and it turned out to be one of the toughest games we'd played all season. Boothy scored the only goal, but we needed all our experience to edge past Peterborough, who had played well above themselves. There was a real sense of belief within the club and it was refreshing to be playing with such freedom. We followed the Cup win by beating United 1–0 at Maine Road and with our top-flight status assured, bar a major capitulation, we could concentrate on getting to our second semi-final of the season. But first we had to see off Everton at Goodison Park. We drew 2–2, thanks to a late Gerry Gow equaliser, and then saw them off 3–1 in the replay, with Bobby McDonald scoring twice in two minutes. Bobby was one of the most attack-minded full backs I'd ever played with and a threat from any set piece because he wasn't afraid to throw himself in where it hurt. John Bond knew the near post was a vulnerable area for most teams and his tactic of playing corners into that area so they could be flicked across the face of the goal – almost impossible to defend against – worked brilliantly and more often than not, it would be Bobby on the end of them. We practised the same drill over and over in training and we became very effective at it. Having players like Tommy Hutchison and Dennis Tueart to deliver perfect crosses helped enormously and if you gave Hutch half a yard he'd whip the ball in at pace for our strikers.

It was full steam ahead to the FA Cup semi-final against Ipswich

Town at Villa Park. It turned out to be an unforgettable day, though we were expected to lose against a fabulous side containing the likes of Paul Cooper, Mick Mills, Alan Brazil, Arnold Muhren, Paul Mariner and John Wark. Ipswich were also involved in the race for the league title, so their pedigree was never in question. We played magnificently on the day but when Paul Power stepped up to take a free-kick in extra time, I wasn't expecting too much. I was wrong; it turned out to be a goal fit to win any game, as he curled the ball into the top corner with his left peg. It was just a shock that Paul had scored it. I can't ever remember him scoring one before or after from a free kick, but thank God he did that day. We ran over to our fans in the Holte End and celebrated with them. It was breathtaking, an unforgettable moment, and the memory of that day that still makes the hairs on the back of my neck stand up.

I hadn't had that much to do during the game and afterwards I saw my mate Paul Mariner in the players' lounge. He said, 'You let us down today, Joe.' I asked him what he meant and he replied: 'Bobby Robson told us to get in as many shots as we could in on you, because according to him, you've gone and you're not the keeper you once were.' He shook his head and smiled because he clearly thought of his manager's statement as no more than psychology, at least I hope that is the case. Beating Ipswich had been an amazing achievement and as I chatted to reporters and the BBC after the game, it hit home just how far we'd come. What better way is there to end a fantastic season than with the greatest game in club football? We were going to Wembley for the FA Cup final.

16

Wembley '81 and *that* Goal

Somebody didn't read the script for the 1981 FA Cup final against Tottenham. If ever a team's name was on the old trophy, it was City's, yet we ended up devastated and unable to believe we'd not rounded off an incredible season by winning the Cup. John Bond said to me, 'You've not just got the game to consider, this is an FA Cup Final – the centenary final – and you'll have to organise a player's committee, a player's pool and you're going to have to talk regularly with the press.' Dennis Tueart, Tommy Hutchison, Paul Power and I formed a committee of sorts and we discussed everything: cameras on our coach; ticket allocation; a rota for players to talk to the press. It was a distraction, something that would never happen today because it's all done for you, but it was interesting at the time.

It's fair to say we took our eye off the ball in the league matches leading up to Wembley and our form going into the final wasn't actually that good, having won just two of our previous nine games, but that was understandable considering the prize on offer and the fact that everyone wanted to stay injury-free.

Our preparations for the final were good, but I wasn't happy with our base in London – the Selsden hotel – because that's where we stayed for the 1974 League Cup final, and, being so bloody superstitious, that to me was a bad omen. That wasn't the team's decision, it was one the club made for us and it surprised me considering we'd had a miserable time on our last visit. The facilities there were superb and the hotel was excellent, but the fact was that Wolves – who we could have been playing had Spurs not seen them off in the semi-final – had beaten us when we last stayed there.

During the build-up to the final, there was a sponsor's dinner at the hotel. Bob Monkhouse was the guest speaker and he was superb. Sharp, witty and intelligent, he had us in stitches but by ten-thirty we were tucked up in bed on the orders of John Bond. Fate was to play a big part in the 1981 final and during our penultimate training session on the Thursday before the match, Bond pondered putting a defender on the post for Glenn Hoddle's free kicks but I was against it. I always thought if a player could curl a ball over a wall and into the top corner, you had to hold your hands up and acknowledge a magnificent piece of skill. The wall was to protect one part of the goal and my job was to cover the rest and as a team we agreed it was best not to put a defender on the line.

On the morning of the final I stuck to my usual routine and went for an hour-long training session with Glyn Pardoe – now a youth-team coach – and Roy Bailey in the hotel grounds. Then it was breakfast before travelling to Wembley stadium. The media were everywhere and were a real distraction. There were sponsors all over the place, too, and the demands on the players were intense. I became acutely aware of how things had changed since the last time we'd been at Wembley with City. In fact, this was around the time that things really began to change in football; the press, television and radio were in your face more than ever before but it was becoming part and parcel of the game, especially for a match that was then the biggest domestic final in world football. Money was pouring into the game and if wages were rising for players, we had to earn them.

I've never played in a World Cup final, but I imagine there can't be many greater occasions than being part of an FA Cup final, at least that's how most players felt back then when it was everyone's boyhood dream. Everything about the day, from the journey from the hotel to the first sight of the Twin Towers took your breath away. Walking down the tunnel and coming out to the roar and a sea of blue-and-white flags was an indescribable feeling. This was what our supporters deserved and their loyalty was being rewarded with a showpiece occasion. Despite the lean years we'd been through, they'd stuck behind us steadfastly and they were making the most of the day. We'd come a long way together, through a time that would have ended with an inevitable parting of the ways nine times out of ten. On a personal level they not only trusted me implicitly, but also they expected me to all but win games by keeping out anything the opposition could throw at me. It was a complete and total turnaround and it might have taken a while but it felt bloody good. I'd gone from zero to hero and I was proud of the supporters and proud of myself. They believed I was England's number one. If only they could have picked the England team.

The 1981 final was a fantastic spectacle and going ahead through Tommy Hutchison's wonderful diving header gave us the edge for most of the game. Then came the fateful moment when Spurs were awarded a very dubious free kick just outside the box. I lined up the wall and was happy there was no way I'd be beaten from that angle or distance. I was prepared for Hoddle to do his worst. There was about ten minutes left, and Hutch, who was on the end of our wall, thought he overheard Hoddle say that he was planning to curl it around the right side of the wall. So, at the last second, he peeled off to block the shot. In fact it was Osvaldo Ardiles who took the kick, which he slid to Hoddle. Hoddle unleashed a shot, and I know I would have either caught it or watched it curl around the post. But fate had a different plan, and, instead, Hutch managed to connect with the ball and deflected it into the opposite corner of the goal for the equaliser. I picked the ball out of the net and belted it towards the centre circle. Hutch was still crouching down, crestfallen. I patted him on the backside and said, 'Come on, we've still got enough time to win this, let's get on with it.' He said he didn't want to, but with a little more encouragement he got up and walked back towards the centre, head still bowed. Hoddle said later it was going in anyway, but it wasn't; it was a freak goal, though I'll never be able to prove it.

At least we hadn't lost, and, despite Paul Miller and Garth Crooks almost putting me on a stretcher with what I thought were a couple of questionable challenges, I survived unscathed and fit for the replay. I felt so sorry for Hutch and Gerry Gow because they'd played their hearts out. Yet Gerry, who'd covered every blade of grass, had given the free kick away that led to the Hoddle free kick, while Hutch was credited with an own goal. In fact I felt sorry for the whole team because it was a match that we dominated from the off. For me, the game should have been settled on the Saturday because that's FA Cup-final day and I did wonder whether our chance had passed us by. The Queen Mother, whom it was a privilege to meet, was guest of honour, along with 100,000 fans and although I don't agree with penalties, I felt it was wrong to replay a game of that stature. England were playing Brazil on the following Wednesday, meaning we couldn't replay the match until the Thursday, which was, to my mind, ridiculous and grossly unfair on the City fans. They would not only have to travel down on a weekday afternoon, but they'd also have to find money to cover the ticket and expenses and head back to Manchester in the early hours of Friday morning. But, I suppose, if we had won, nobody would have cared.

We travelled down to London the day before the replay and a few of the lads were struggling with injury and fatigue, particularly Gerry Gow. Spurs had a younger squad, though arguably we were the fitter side, but we still felt deflated from not winning the game on the Saturday, mainly because we had been by far the better side. It was a strange day and was in fact the first time an FA Cup final had been replayed at Wembley.

I'm still amazed that 40,000 City fans made their way to London for the second time in six days, but it just didn't feel like an FA Cup final to me, but then maybe all replayed finals felt like that. We soon fell behind to a Ricky Villa goal but Steve Mackenzie's equaliser – a twenty-five-yard volley into the top corner – was one of the best goals I've ever seen and I was delighted it was Hutch who laid off the ball with an intelligent header. Then we went 2–1 up in the second half through a Kevin Reeves penalty and that was the time I felt we should have brought Dennis Tueart on because he had the experience of playing in cup finals and was unlucky not to start. It would have been excellent timing and taken the wind out of any potential Spurs fight back. We had chances to kill the game off, but Ricky Villa – whom I'd been disgusted with in the first game for the way he huffily sloped off the pitch after being substituted – would have a huge part to play in the remaining minutes. Garth Crooks equalised as Spurs went for broke and they got the winner shortly after with a goal that is still talked about as one of the greatest ever scored in an FA Cup final. But what people don't realise is that it had more than one touch of good fortune about it.

In the seventy-seventh minute Villa set off on a mazy run about twenty-five yards out and our defenders seemed scared to put in a challenge in case they gave away a penalty. Within a few moments, he was through and approaching my goal. He dropped a shoulder, touched the ball on – in my view accidentally – and I thought that was my chance and lunged towards him. However, as soon as I made my move, I realised it was a mistake because he was going to beat me to the ball. His momentum had peaked at the perfect moment and it was too late to do anything about it and he poked the ball underneath my body and into the net. There was a moment's silence and then the Spurs fans went bananas. The dream was over. There had been chances for Ray Ranson to clear the ball, and, nine times out of ten, he would have done, but on this occasion he didn't and nobody else did, either. Nobody was to blame because it was a good goal, even if his last touch was a toe-poke. It was typical of the way things had gone during the match that we should lose in such dramatic circumstances.

We were devastated, but we could at least say we'd taken part in two of the best FA Cup finals ever. Bob Wilson approached me as I walked off and said, 'I can't believe you lost that game, Joe.' He wasn't alone, either. Ironically, the BBC selected me as man-of-the-match for both games. I popped my head into the Tottenham dressing room, congratulated them and wished them well for the European Cup Winners Cup final, which they were due to play a week or so later, but did so with a heavy heart. The next day we left our hotel and as we made our way down the M1, we caught sight of Wembley. Tommy Hutchison sighed and said, 'I'm never going to go back there. I hate the place.' It was sad because Tommy didn't deserve what had happened to him; none of the lads did. It had been an incredible journey and when we got over our disappointment, we began looking forward to the new season, wondering if the momentum could be maintained.

I'm certain the club made a fair bit of money from our two Wembley trips, but there didn't seem to be much of a transfer kitty for John Bond. There were rumours of one or two big names coming to Maine Road, but none of us were privy to their identity. We returned for training in preparation for the 1981/82 season with many people tipping us as dark horses for Europe or even a trophy. No doubt our own supporters would expect us to push on, too and we couldn't possibly start off as badly as we had done during the previous year. We'd shown that we were capable of beating anyone and all we had to do was keep playing the way we had.

Tottenham must have been impressed with my displays during the cup finals because during the pre-season I was informed through the grapevine that they wanted to sign me. Spurs lodged a formal bid with City and I went to see John Bond to see what was happening. He advised me I should speak to the chairman, which I did, and Peter Swales told me there had been no offers and even if there had have been, I wouldn't be allowed to go. My ties to City were still strong and I'd seen enough during the previous campaign to suggest we could really go places. The club obviously shared that belief by buying Trevor Francis, a man I believed was the best striker in the country. I'd known Trevor for a while through England and he was a quiet, unassuming man with no airs or graces. The £1 million price tag was well deserved because he had a Rolls Royce engine purring beneath his shirt. While supporters had questioned Steve Daley's fee, nobody complained about Trevor's. He immediately became our highest-paid player, though I was being looked after financially by the club and it was therefore never a problem. I'm not sure I could say the same for some of the other first-team players, who I think weren't too happy about the wage gap, but it was up to them to fight their own corners.

I felt we still needed a goal-scoring midfielder if we wanted to push for a place in the top six. However, with Francis in the side, we now had that extra touch of class up front and all the pieces of the Bond jigsaw seemed to be falling into place. There was a good blend of youth and experience and in addition Asa Hartford rejoined City following a couple of years at Nottingham Forest and Everton; just as Dennis Tueart's return had given us a shot in the arm, so would Asa's. They had both left Maine Road at their peak and while it's never easy to go back and have the same kind of impact, I feel both players managed to do that during their second spells.

Asa had probably been one of the main reasons Gerry Gow never won a full Scotland cap during the Seventies, and, ironically, his return would now threaten Gerry's future at City. I loved Gerry to bits: he was a down-to-earth bloke, and someone who, despite his physique, you wouldn't want to mess with. He had been a terrier for us but all the crunching tackles he'd made, and all the balls he'd won that he had no right to win, had taken a toll on his ankles and knees. Two months into the new campaign he was ruled out for a while and would never play for the club again. I could see Tommy Hutchison had lost some of his spark and he would also leave the club this season.

John Bond brought his son Kevin in from Norwich. I was very surprised by that decision because it was never going to be easy for either of them. If things went badly, there would be accusations of nepotism and of Kevin being a 'daddy's boy'. I wasn't sure Kevin or another signing, Norwegian defender Aage Hareide, were of the calibre needed to take the club forward. I had a feeling that Trevor's arrival had emptied the coffers and that there was nothing left in the pot.

Still, we flew out of the blocks and by Christmas 1981 we were mounting a decent title challenge. We managed to carry on the feel-good factor from the previous campaign and we travelled to Anfield on Boxing Day full of confidence and ready to take them on in their own backyard. On the day, we were excellent and outplayed Liverpool completely, going 3–1 up through Kevin Reeves. I was at the Kop end for that goal and as I walked back towards my line from the edge of the box, something hit me on the head, poleaxing me completely. I didn't know what had happened and was stunned for a few moments before Roy Bailey ran on to assist me. I'd had a lot of things thrown at me during my career, but I had never been hit on the head. From what I can gather the object that hit me was a wine bottle. I was okay and I as I got up again, the Kop were absolutely brilliant, applauding me and even singing, 'England, England's Number One!' which I appreciated. I heard that the Liverpool fans, with whom I'd always enjoyed good banter, sorted out the guy who'd thrown the bottle, which wouldn't surprise me at all. They were proud of being a sporting bunch and wouldn't have taken kindly to the actions of one idiot threatening their reputation.

Afterwards the police asked me if I wanted to press charges against Liverpool – the home club being responsible for security – but I had no intention of going down that road. As far as I was concerned it had been an isolated incident and I didn't want to take things any further. The day after it happened, there was a report that the wine bottle had been lying in the back of the net for some time, alongside a small miniature of whisky. There were claims that it had been the smaller bottle that had hit me and that left a sour taste in my mouth because I'd taken a real whack. One of the lads said they knew it had been the bigger bottle because it had been full when it hit my head and empty by the time it hit the ground.

A reporter from the *Daily Express* wrote several articles over the next week, asking why Liverpool hadn't been taken to task about the incident but I just wanted to let it go. There had been no serious damage done and it was time to move on. Curiously, I was later told that Liverpool made an enquiry to buy me immediately after that match having been less than impressed by their own keeper – Bruce Grobbelaar – but they weren't given any encouragement by City, who told them 'nothing doing'. It's worth remembering we were above them in the table by that point, so it's hardly surprising. Would I have signed for them if asked? I'm not sure – it would have been a wrench to leave City but if I had gone anywhere, Anfield would have been very high on a very short list.

We followed up the victory over Liverpool by beating Wolves two days later at Maine Road to go top of the table. We couldn't have gone into the New Year on much more of a high and eased past Cardiff in the FA Cup third round with another comfortable-looking tie to come in the next round, against Coventry at Maine Road. It was all set up for us to power on to Wembley and maybe this time come home with the trophy, but things were about to go pear-shaped. Perhaps we believed Coventry, who had lost on eight successive visits to our place, would present no real challenge and if that really was the case, then more fool us. We were comprehensively beaten 3–1 and I was even chipped for one of the goals, so as you can imagine I wasn't a happy chap. Another shot hit a small divot I'd made for goal kicks and as I dived for a low shot it hit the divot and bounced over me and into the net. It just wasn't our day and as I walked off towards the tunnel, a bloke shouted down from the main stand, 'Corrigan you useless bastard!' I admit that I lost it and ran into the stands to try and catch him, but he managed to get away which, in the mood I was in, was his good fortune. It had been a hugely disappointing day and both the fans and the team had been thinking about a return trip to Wembley so I could understand the frustration. What nobody could have envisaged was the sapping effect that result had on the rest of our season. It was incredible and we won just five of our remaining twenty league games and slid from top to a final league position of tenth.

Trevor Francis had been brilliant for us when he played, but he spent too much time in the treatment room and having lost Dennis Tueart with a snapped Achilles, and seen both Hutch and Gow leave the club, we faded badly and that didn't bode well for the future.

Despite the flat end to the second half of the season, I at least could look forward to the 1982 World Cup in Spain and it was just a pity I couldn't have gone to it with a spring in my step. I was hoping against hope that I might be selected for one or two games, but, as it turned out, the experience would leave me feeling disillusioned. I don't think I could have been any more patient than I had been despite promises being made to me that were never kept. As I was now in my thirties, I thought this would almost certainly be my last major tournament with England. I'd never been given a run in the team and the pleas in the media over the years from the likes of John Bond, Tony Book and Malcolm Allison had fallen on deaf ears. What I didn't know was that a meeting had been held with the England management, during which Peter Shilton had told them that he was fed up with the rotation between him and Clemence and that if they didn't make him the first choice, he wasn't going to go to the World Cup. Clem had been a regular starter up to that point and there was no reason to drop him because he had done nothing wrong. What really hurt was that I was disregarded totally. It appeared, more than ever before, that politics played as much a part in the selection process as form at club level. I knew I was third choice, but I always went out with the intention of being number one so that I was prepared if called upon.

We progressed through the first phase after some impressive per- formances, particularly against France, and Peter Withe and I organised a qualification party at the hotel with the intention of a smallish get- together, though it ended up as anything but. The following day I was training when I heard a loud crack in my knee. It wasn't painful but the doctor told me I'd torn my cartilage and had to go home. I called Dr Luft at City and he arranged for me to see a specialist in Manchester. I left the England party behind and reluctantly flew home. Gary Bailey was set to replace me in the squad but FIFA wouldn't allow any replace- ments at that late stage. In the meantime, I had my knee examined and was told there was nothing wrong with it and was fine to resume training. There was no swelling and no soreness so I flew to the new base in Madrid, but still ended up watching the games from the stands in the searing Spanish heat. We reached the quarter-final and didn't lose a game, but that was my last involvement with the senior England squad. It was hardly surprising when you consider who took over from Ron Greenwood: Bobby Robson, the man who told his Ipswich players that 'Joe had gone' prior to the 1981 FA Cup semi-final, although to his credit, he called me and said he wanted me to be one of the senior pros on an England B tour to Australia the following summer.

17

Lost in America

There was, once again, no investment during the close season. John Bond, who looked to me to be nearing the end of his tether, was reduced to bringing in loan players and free transfers. Perhaps not surprisingly, the 1982/83 campaign would be nothing short of disastrous. Little did I know that not only Bond would be out of the door before the season reached its dreadful climax, but also that I'd be gone. John Sainty had left the club and losing such a talented coach was bound to have a negative effect. The players loved him and he had played a big part in the success we had enjoyed under Bond.

I was thirty-three, so not getting any younger, though I was still flying around in training and had never felt fitter. The emergence of Alex Williams was keeping me on my toes and I knew there was a real possibility this could be my last season at Maine Road. Alex was a great kid who had waited patiently for his opportunity and due to various injuries that I'd sustained over the previous two years, he had already played five times for the first team by the time he was called upon for his first real run in the side. I trained with him every day and had done since he was a youth-team player so I knew if I was out for any amount of time, he'd make it hard for me to win back my place. I enjoyed the challenge and needed it, following Keith MacRae's departure a couple of years earlier. He was a lovely kid from a lovely family and a very humble young man.

There was one new arrival who might have been an asset to the squad: Northern Ireland international Martin O'Neill, who had joined the club during the summer from Nottingham Forest. Martin was a bundle of nervous energy and ended up receiving a dose of Corrigan justice after being set-up by the rest of the lads. We travelled down to the West Country for a pre-season friendly with Bideford, and, during a training session, a few of the lads told Martin that I liked being chipped when I was off my line because it kept me on my toes, especially if it came out of the blue. I'm not sure why anyone would believe that, but, during the session, the ball fell to Martin, and, sure enough, he chipped the ball over my head and into the net. I wasn't happy. Later that day we beat Bideford 4–1 and the next morning, after we got on the team coach and as I passed Martin, I aimed a jab at his shoulder as pay back. I missed and ended up hitting him in the chest, breaking one of his ribs. Funnily enough, he never tried it again. We flew off to Germany shortly after and were given a real hammering by Werder Bremen, who beat us 8–0. It was the heaviest defeat of my professional career and at one point the referee ran up to me and told me to release the ball quicker. We were 5–0 down and I asked him for a bit of mercy, saying that it was the only time I'd been able to hold the ball other than to pick it out of the back of the net. Prior to the game there had been a delay at the hotel as we waited to set off. I got off to look for John Bond and John Benson and was told there had been a phone call from England from Peter Swales. I got back on the coach and told the lads; fifteen minutes later Bond returned and asked the driver to get off for a few minutes and to close the door behind him, which he did. It all seemed pretty ominous, then he then said, 'Lads, I've just had a call from the chairman. We are trying to buy a player from Southampton but there's no money available. The chairman has asked me to ask you if you'd be willing to delay any bonuses due to you this season for twelve months so we can bring in Graham Baker.' He then said he'd get off the coach for ten minutes while we made up our minds.

It took about five seconds for me to make my mind up. It was totally unacceptable that the club should even think about asking us to do something like that. There were one or two murmurings among the lads so I got up and said, 'Look, I've never heard anything like that before in my career. I don't think it's the right thing to do because how do we know those bonuses will ever be paid?' I said I wasn't going to give up my bonuses, but apparently a lot of the others were willing to do just that. It didn't seem right to me. I had to think of my family and I don't think my stance was unreasonable.

Trevor Francis had been sold in the summer and you had to wonder where the money from his sale had gone. It showed the club was setting its sights lower and lower, with survival the only target, either that or the debts were becoming unsustainable. Despite the financial situation, Graham Baker signed and looked a decent player. We actually won our first two games before taking on Watford at Maine Road. There were only a few minutes on the clock when I went for a cross with Nigel Callaghan who caught me with a boot in the face, just under my nose, and cracked a bone. As I'd been flying through the air at the time, I landed badly and broke my collarbone. I'd wanted to play on but Roy Bailey said there was no chance and Bobby McDonald had to go in goal instead. We won 1–0, with Bobby doing a passable impression of Superman for the remainder of the game. The win put us top of the table, but we were only papering over the cracks.

I had to go to hospital to have a special strapping put over my shoulder and under my arm. I was in more pain from the strapping than I was from my collarbone injury, but, unbeknown to me or to the nurse who strapped me up, I had some floating fragments of bone in my elbow and the pressure from the bandaging was agonising. They were dosing me up on painkillers and later that evening a couple of friends and Val came to visit me and they had brought a couple of bottles of wine with them, which of course I couldn't drink. They enjoyed themselves, though. I was told I might need my collarbone pinned and one of the nurses told me they'd been unable to contact the club surgeon, David Markham, and that I would be operated on the following morning. They told me that the club had given permission for the operation but moments before I was due to go into the theatre, the doors burst open and David Markham, the club's orthopaedic surgeon, came in and demanded to know what was happening. The nurse told him and he said, 'No. That's not going to happen. He needs rehabilitation, not an operation.' He then explained that if I had undergone surgery I would have been left with a frozen shoulder, effectively ending my career. It took six weeks of intensive work with Roy Bailey to get back to full fitness. During that time, Alex Williams proved himself to be a top-class goalkeeper and perhaps showed that the club could live without Joe Corrigan, if the situation demanded. I was still considered first choice by Bond, and returned for the Manchester derby at Old Trafford, but felt my position had been weakened by the events of the past few months. Our league form was patchy to say the least though we were mid-table and had progressed through to the fourth round of the FA Cup where we would play Brighton at the Goldstone Ground, a match that would have a dramatic impact on the remaining months of the season.

In the previous round we'd seen off Sunderland after a replay but a Sunday-morning training session at Maine Road prior to the game showed how badly things had deteriorated at the club and should have made the events after the game at Brighton not quite so surprising. As we trained, Nicky Reid and John Bond had an argument that had threatened to get out of hand, and that resulted in a nasty half hour of action with some players intent on hurting one another. Something wasn't right and it later transpired that Bond had received a £500,000 bid for Reid that had been quashed at boardroom level; Bond, I believe, had earmarked that money to rebuild his faltering squad.

Brighton hammered us 4–0 in the cup-tie. It was a dreadful day and an awful, disjointed performance by all of us. As we left the pitch Alex Williams walked over to console me and I said, 'It's yours now kid. I won't be here for much longer.'

'What do you mean by that?' he asked. I explained that the cup exit would mean cost-cutting exercises and I'd be one of them. I assured him I would be on my way before long and, within three months, that's exactly what happened.

John Bond resigned after that game and I think the Nicky Reid incident might have had something to do with it; that plus the chronic lack of funds probably tipped him over the edge. He'd done a great job for City but the club weren't backing him. In fact, things had got so bad that little Jimmy Rous, the kit man, was told that he wasn't allowed to throw plastic bin bags away; he had to empty them into a bigger bag and reuse them. We'd clearly slipped into a very precarious position and it was obvious where the club was headed.

John Benson took over from Bond and although I had a great deal of respect for him, his appointment should have been for a couple of weeks at best because he didn't have the experience of managing a team, especially one that was in freefall. Our form was poor and though there was still daylight between us and the bottom three, that could change. Benson would have been the first to hold his hands up that the immense pressure he was under was too much to cope with. The truth, with the greatest respect, was that he was the cheapest option available and if things didn't work out and he had to be sacked, the compensation would be minimal.

It was not long after the Brighton game that I first heard rumblings about interest in me from American club Seattle Sounders. Tony Penman, an agent for Nike, had approached me about playing in the States when I ran a training clinic with Bob Wilson – the first recognised goalkeeper coach in England – in Seattle. When he asked, I was still an integral part of City's first team but the rumours persisted, albeit without any official approach. Then, after we'd lost at Swansea City, stories appeared in the press, saying I was on my way. This time, I went to see Peter Swales and asked him what was going on.

'I don't understand the question,' he said.

I asked him whether I was being transferred or not, but he denied any knowledge of it. The reports in the press led to Chelsea registering their interest, saying they wanted to buy me if I became available so things appeared to be moving quickly.

'Am I staying or going on the transfer list?' I asked.

'That's up to you,' Swales replied.

'That means I'm going, then.'

Swales asked why I'd come to that conclusion and I told him that whenever I'd asked that question in the past, the answer had always been 'you're going nowhere'. Now I sensed a shift in attitude. I said he'd just proved he didn't want me at the club any more by his answer to my question. That's how my future was decided and it wasn't anything to do with me going to the chairman and demanding a transfer because I would have stayed if he had said what he'd always said previously. The fact was my questions just brought matters to a head. A meeting was arranged with John Benson and Tony Penman when John Bond walks in out of the blue to say that he was part of the negotiations. I said, 'This isn't right. I'm not even sure if I'm going yet.' As it was, I reached an agreement with Seattle shortly after and just a couple of weeks after confronting the chairman, I was gone.

Val and the kids were excited at the prospect of living in America, but I was disappointed at leaving City after sixteen years, particularly when I felt I still had a lot to offer the club. City gave me a golden hand-shake of £30,000, but I later found out that Seattle had in fact paid that amount for me. I was devastated that the club had asked for a fee because I'd been told that, due to the poor turnout at my testimonial, they'd give me a termination payment when I retired or moved on. I'm not complaining because I earned decent money in my later years at Maine Road, but the fact that they wanted to recoup my golden handshake by asking for a fee meant that, in my eyes, I was being paid nothing by the club at which I'd spent most of my life. It left a bitter taste. We'd been through a lot together and it hurt.

I was scheduled to fly out on 3 April 1983 and Big Helen and a large number of City fans turned up at the airport to see us off on our new adventure. It was a wonderful gesture, one I'll never forget, but with the house sold in Sale, we uprooted and headed for a new life in the States. Val could have stayed in England with the kids, but we'd decided to stick together as a family and make a real go of it. Bruce Anderson, Seattle's owner, set everything up and as we took off I could see Big Helen on top of the car park with a flag saying 'Good luck Joe'. The other supporters were beside her, waving us off. It was a lovely way to leave Manchester and it vindicated my decision to turn down a substantial amount of money from a tabloid newspaper to dish the dirt on the club. I always wanted to be able to return Maine Road one day and be able to hold my head up high, whether as a visitor or otherwise.

As the plane set down in Seattle, it immediately felt like we'd done the right thing. There was a Buddhist convention in Portland and the Corrigan clan had been sitting amidst a sea of orange on the plane going over; I felt like I was travelling to watch Holland.

I had to use my holiday visa to get into the country because Seattle hadn't sorted out the documentation needed for employment. Then, as we entered the terminal, Val and I were dragged into a room with the kids forced to wait outside while we were given the third degree by an immigration officer. They had been alerted to the true purpose of my visit by a story in the American press, and told us in no uncertain terms that we weren't being allowed into the country because I didn't have the correct visas. We'd been assured it would be okay by the owner and manager of Seattle, but we got a bit of a fright until the immigration people changed their minds and let us in on the tourist visas. With a sigh of relief we came out into an empty arrivals hall. Our kids had hauled off the luggage themselves and were patiently waiting for us. It was some start to our new life.

Steve Daley, Peter Ward, John Ryan and Kevin Bond – all now playing in the NASL – came along to welcome us at the airport and it was nice to see some friendly faces after our ordeal. Seattle was beautiful and our new home was at the bottom of the Cascade Mountains. The people were kind and it was one of the nicest places you could imagine living. There was also a strong ex-pat community, mostly players, and we felt at home very quickly. We rented initially, but soon found a place we wanted to own and so bought a palatial new home for around $100,000, not perhaps the wisest decision considering the fragile state of the NASL, but we were determined to make a success of life in America. Our whole way of life and standard of living went up a couple of notches and there was no pressure on the playing side of things. I wanted to help make an impact over there and do my bit to take the game up to the next level. In addition, the US was gunning for the 1986 World Cup, a wonderful prospect, and it would probably have saved the NASL had the bid been successful. When it was awarded to Colombia instead, their enthusiasm faded and people quickly lost interest in football. Even when Colombia suffered an earthquake and were not able to fulfil their commitment, FIFA gave it to Mexico. It was like rubbing their noses in the dirt twice and it sent out a message that the USA were way off FIFA's radar.

It was a real shame. The kids in America loved football, primarily because anyone could take part, but the dads who took them to the game didn't have a clue what the rules were and didn't want to have a seven-year-old explaining them. At a fans' forum I attended, people said that they were ignoring the appeals to come and watch the Sounders because they'd rather spend their money watching basketball, baseball or American football. Why would they want to pay to watch second-class soccer played by ageing foreigners? I even had to start phoning lapsed season-ticket holders to try and get them to come back, but they weren't interested.

Fans deserted Seattle in their droves and teams across the country were folding left, right and centre. We wanted to coach kids and promote the game, but we were probably two years too late. I was immersed in my new life when I got a phone call from an English journalist who was in the States to ask if he could do an article with me for the Friday papers about City's last game of the season. I agreed and met him on a local pier with the waves crashing under our feet. Manchester was the last thing on my mind so I was taken aback when the first thing he asked me was whether I was aware that City needed a draw against Luton to stay up. I couldn't believe it. I hadn't even thought about City because they'd been safe when I left; yet now, they were within a point of relegation. I believed they were too good to go down, a fatal assumption as it turned out, and told the journalist as much. The next day we had a game in Seattle's stadium, the King Dome, and as we were getting ready to run out, Steve Daley came in and told us City had been relegated. I was devastated and didn't understand what had gone on, but I should have realised it was a possibility. The team had been in a downward spiral since the Christmas of the previous season and by the time they finally dropped into the bottom three it was too late to do anything about it. I felt so sorry for Alex Williams, who was blamed by some for the goal Luton scored but it wasn't his fault; besides, the damage had been done long before.

Of course, I had my own concerns and when Bruce Anderson told us Seattle were struggling financially, it brought back memories of my last few months at City. I thought 'here we go again'. Anderson tried to secure a place for the team in the US Indoor Soccer League, which was then quite lucrative and reasonably popular. It would have seen us through the winter, but it didn't materialise. To add to my worries, we'd bought a house and sold our English home, so we were in complete limbo; maybe we should have rented after all. By the time I received a call to say that Seattle were folding, I wished I had. It had all happened so quickly and returning home was our only option. I was offered a chance to play for a club in Hong Kong but when they asked what my wage was at Seattle, they went quiet and never called back.

Derby County enquired, but they couldn't pay my wages either. Fortunately, Seattle manager Laurie Calloway then called to ask if I wanted to go home. He told me that Brighton – who'd just lost the FA Cup final against Manchester United and been relegated – were very interested. In truth, I wanted to stay in America, but there didn't seem to be any other choice. New York Cosmos and San Diego wanted to take on my contract, which could be assigned to a new club after a certain date, but that date was later than the potential start date at Brighton so I had to make a decision. I needed security for my wife and kids so despite the lure of the States I took the safe option. We packed up and flew home to begin another new chapter, this time on the south coast of England. It turned out I'd made the right choice, because within a year the NASL had collapsed. Had I stayed I would simply have been delaying the inevitable.

I'd had a marvellous stay in America, albeit a brief one, but if I had the chance to do it all again, I would. I had not been paid for several weeks due to Seattle's dire financial situation but an agreement was struck with Brighton that they would pay a fee that would then be transferred into my bank account for the wages I was owed. Some of the money also went to pay what some of the other lads were owed, but I don't know if they got their full whack.

18

Brighton Rock

I returned to England in September 1983 ready to begin life as a Brighton player. It would be the first time I'd played for a club outside the top flight having never actually seen any first-team action during my loan spell at Shrewsbury. They had the makings of a decent squad and most people felt we could bounce back to the top flight at the first attempt. It was a beautiful place to live, but completely different to life in Manchester. I'd come from an area where you could nip down to the local and have a pint on your own if you felt like it. At the same time, you were never lonely as punters would always come up and talk about City. It was much more standoffish in Sussex, where, if you went out on your own, you probably wouldn't talk to a soul. Neither Val nor I knew anyone in Brighton apart from the players and so we decided to rent a house in Hove rather than diving in feet first and buying a place.

The sea was five minutes away and we enrolled the kids at an excellent local school, so, off the pitch, everything was great, which, as any player will tell you, is just as important as everything being right on it. I had always negotiated my own contracts so when I sat down with chairman Mike Bamber and manager Jimmy Melia, I was surprised that Jimmy was asked to leave the room before we began to discuss my terms. For some reason, I asked the chairman what would happen if I was badly injured. What would happen to my wages? He asked me why I asked that and I didn't really know the answer but he added, 'Don't worry about it, Joe. We'll insure you for £100,000.' That was the first time I'd really heard of insurance policies on players, but it would turn out to be a question well worth asking, though I'm still not sure why I'd asked in the first place.

Jimmy Melia was sacked shortly after I'd signed my contract – maybe that's why he'd been excluded from the negotiations – and Chris Catlin took over. He was a former Coventry City left back and would turn out to be the worst manager I'd ever played under. However, at thirty-five, I knew I just had to work hard and do my best. It hadn't seemed like I'd been back five minutes and already I was on my way back to Maine Road, this time in the colours of another team, which would be very strange. I flew up to Manchester before the rest of the team travelled so I could spend some time with my mum and dad and then I met up with the squad at a Manchester-airport hotel and we were soon setting off for Moss Side.

The drive along Princess Parkway was surreal and I kept away from the windows, trying to keep my emotions in check. When I got off the bus I got a lovely reception from the fans around the main entrance and all the old feelings started to flood back, though it was a bit odd getting changed in the away dressing room. Finally, it was time to walk down the tunnel and as soon as I stepped on to the pitch I was greeted by the most wonderful standing ovation from the entire ground. It seemed to go on for an age. It was incredible and brought a lump to my throat. I'd never been able to say goodbye properly to the City supporters, so this was a special moment for me and it also meant a lot more to me than any testimonial match. I went to see Big Helen, just like the old days, but I think the rest of the Brighton team may have lost their focus in the emotion of the occasion and we didn't perform at all on the day, going down 4–0.

After the match, I gave a press interview and said that I hoped this was the dawn of a new era for the club and also that I hoped the manager, who was Billy McNeill at the time, would get financial backing because a club like Manchester City shouldn't be a division-two side. I wanted nothing but success for those wonderful fans and even thinking about my homecoming game still chokes me. City fans always remember their favourite players and, if you've done right by them, they'll stand by you no matter who you played for – well, with maybe one exception!

Playing for Brighton felt a little like being on holiday. It was by the sea, we were renting a home and the players had a different attitude. The lads enjoyed a good social life and I felt things weren't as focused as they should have been, but whether that was down to the division we were in, the lads at the club or the manager, I'm not sure, though Catlin was certainly part of the reason. He owned a rock shop in the town and also had a home in Brighton so whether that swung the job for him, I don't know. He brought in former Arsenal player Sammy Nelson as his right-hand man. Catlin just didn't have the right character to manage, in my opinion, and things deteriorated pretty quickly during his tenure. We had players like Steve Gatting, Steve Foster, Jimmy Case, Tony Grealish and Gordon Smith – a terrific bunch of lads – but we lacked direction and drive. It was hard to get used to the smaller crowds at the Goldstone Ground after so many years at Maine Road playing in front of crowds of 40,000 or more, but perhaps if a certain player in had come at the same time as I did, things might have been different.

'Jimmy Melia stitched me up,' chairman Mike Bamber told me. I asked him what he meant and he replied: 'Well he promised me you and Kevin Keegan, but only you turned up.' I thought that Jimmy had probably been sacked because of poor results, not because he'd failed to get Keegan, but it was hard to imagine Kevin ever signing for Brighton.

Our season bumbled along and the return match with City a few months later was also a memorable encounter. I took a whack on my elbow, the one I'd had floating bone in, and was given an injection at half-time and told I'd be going out again, which I'd wanted to do anyway. Again, I got a fabulous reception from the travelling City fans and the match ended one apiece, honours even. I'd signed a three-year deal and the first season passed without much incident or success and I returned to pre-season training hoping that things would pick up and we could have a crack at winning promotion. Then Catlin asked me to meet him in his office shortly after the first training session of the summer.

'I'm just telling you now that you're not going to play for the first team again.'

'Oh,' I replied. 'For what reason?'

'Why? Because I've made my decision and we've decided to go with Perry Digweed this season. In fact, I don't want you here any more and would prefer it if you left the club.'

'Fair enough,' I said. 'You find me a club and I'm gone.'

The main reason, I assumed, was my wages. Getting me off the pay-roll would free up enough cash to pay two or three decent players. I understood it was a business decision and didn't take it personally. Of course, they never came up with anything and so when I was interviewed a little while into the season, I told the reporter in so many words that I was disillusioned with life under Chris Catlin and his attitude towards me, which I found disrespectful and ignorant. After it appeared in the paper, he fined me two weeks' wages for 'going public'. I wasn't having that because all I'd done was spoken the truth and if Catlin didn't like it, so what? He had made it clear I was surplus to requirements so I owed him nothing and I launched a formal appeal, which my union, the Professional Footballer's Association, fully supported. Gordon Taylor, their top man, called me up to tell me they'd had enough and that if managers could speak publicly about players, why shouldn't players be able to speak up when they wanted? It was deja vu because it had happened before at City under Malcolm. As things stood, we were fined every time we opened our mouths.

A tribunal was arranged at FA headquarters in London. Chris Catlin, Gordon Taylor and I were in front of a panel and Gordon was magnificent. He put everything across in a manner that would have been beyond me and despite Brighton's protestations that the ruling would open a can of worms, the panel ruled in my favour. Catlin was livid. 'I can't fucking believe you, Joe,' he said. 'The club will never let this lie.' Whatever he thought, Brighton had to refund my fine. I had got one over on him and I wondered what his reaction would be. I didn't have to wait long to find out.

The day after I received a phone call from Sammy Nelson telling me not to report for training, but to meet him at the ground at 4.30 that afternoon. I said that would be no problem and arrived at the designated time. Only the kit man was there, so I got changed and eventually Nelson turned up and said, 'Right, you've got to run and run and run . . . .'

I told him that was fine by me and began to jog around the pitch as slowly as I possibly could. In my opinion it showed how petty Catlin and company were; they'd obviously spat their dummies out of the pram. It seemed to me they were trying to break my resolve but they couldn't. I'd been through a lot in my career, I was a thirty-five-year-old former England keeper and this was child's play to me, though I admit it was the worst period of my career. It must have taken me three or four minutes to complete the lap and while I was meandering round Sammy was watching me, so I said, 'Look, I'll do what I have to do, but you're going to stand there and watch me until I've finished.' I continued my gentle jog around the Goldstone and took forever to complete the task.

The next morning Catlin hauled me in.

'We're not having that again.'

I retorted, 'Chris, let's get this straight. I'm not twenty-five, I'm thirty-five and coming to the end of my career. I've got a good contract so if you want me to go, find me a club. If you want me to play in the youth team, fine. If you want me in the reserves, I'll play. That's what I'm paid to do – play football. That's what the article was all about: playing for the first team.'

Nothing changed for the next few weeks and I was still training on my own when I got a call to go in and see Catlin again. He told me Norwich wanted to take me on loan and I think I'd packed my bags before he ended the sentence. Ken Brown and Mel Machin were in charge at Carrow Road and they wanted me to replace Chris Woods, who was out injured. It was a breath of fresh air and though I only played four games, it was great to be playing again and to feel wanted. Norwich were in the top flight, too, which was even better. I even played against Tommy Booth's Preston side, where he was player-manager, in the Milk Cup and we beat them 6–1, which Boothy wasn't best pleased with. It was great to catch up with him, though, and we had a good laugh and a drink afterwards. Knowing how nice a person Tom is, I wondered if he was cut out for management, but he gave it a right good go.

I had a terrific month at Carrow Road before having to return to Brighton but fortunately it was only briefly as Stoke City came in for me after Peter Fox injured his back. I went on loan to the Victoria Ground for a month and really enjoyed my stay. The loan period was extended for a second month, though the team were rooted to the bottom of the table. What would turn out to be my last game in the top flight was a 2–1 victory over Manchester United – not a bad way to sign off. Before I left for Brighton, I went to see Stoke manager Bill Asprey who told me he was interested in keeping me for another month and offered to pay a fee as well. I'd been discussing my future with Val and she wasn't happy with me being away from home and from the kids so the move to the

Potteries made a lot of sense. It turned out that Bill was keen to make the move permanent in due course, if the financial issues could be resolved. He explained the problem: 'Joe, we just can't afford your wages, not with a transfer fee on top of that.'

I suggested that he should try and persuade Brighton to settle my contract with them so I could move on a free. It would mean that I was a free agent and he could afford me. I left it in Bill's hands and returned to Brighton, explaining to Catlin that I thought the solution was a move to Stoke. He told me he wanted me to play for the reserves at the weekend against QPR, which was progress of sorts. It meant playing on the artificial pitch at Loftus Road, a place most keepers held in disdain because we suffered more than most diving around on a rock-hard surface. Fate, however, was dealing the cards that afternoon and the only one with a losing hand would be me.

During the game I ran out to intercept a through ball and as I dived the centre forward flipped me up in the air. I landed on my neck and felt a searing pain shoot down my neck and my left side. I managed to carry on until half-time but in the dressing room I told the physio something wasn't right; I could feel a tingling sensation in my hands and my neck was sore. He told me I should be fine and I carried on. On returning home, I told Val about the pain and explained how I'd done it and suddenly I realised that I'd actually landed on my right yet the pain was down my left. The following morning I felt that something was definitely wrong. I sat down at the breakfast table and became aware that my left arm kept flopping down as though it was out of my control. Val drove me into see the physio straight away and he told me I'd have to go and have an x-ray. The results showed I'd burst a disc out of my neck and it had gone into my nervous system and partially paralysed my left side. It was decided I had to have the disc removed and replaced with bone grafted from my hip and that it needed to be done urgently.

After the operation I remember coming around in intensive care and being transferred to a side ward. It was Saturday morning and the television was on. As I lay there with tubes coming out of every imaginable orifice, I watched Bob Wilson on *Football Focus*. He was speaking about the weekend fixtures when he said, 'We've just been informed by Brighton and Hove Albion that Joe Corrigan has had to finish playing football due to injury and our thoughts are with Joe at what must be a difficult time for him.' I nearly went into relapse! I couldn't believe it – I'd just had the operation so how did they know I was finished? How could anyone know? In my view it epitomised my time at Brighton and the methods of certain individuals at the club, which at times beggared belief.

Catlin came to see me two days later and I asked him what he'd been playing at by announcing that I was finished. He admitted it had been 'a bit premature'. I said nobody had told me I was finished but he said that retiring might be the best option for everyone. It then transpired that the insurance company took the view that my injury was due to wear and tear. But Brighton were desperate to cash in on my policy so I could be paid off and weren't about to accept that decision. I was sent to Harley Street, where I was examined by a specialist. His conclusion was that all my other vertebrae were fine and that the injury sustained at Loftus Road, and not wear and tear, had made it impossible for me to carry on playing. If I did, there could be serious consequences because there was a danger of bone being knocked into my spinal chord if I took a further blow to my neck. So time had finally been called on my playing career, maybe a year or two ahead of schedule, but at least I could walk and had undergone a successful operation. All I had to do now was work out what I was going to do with the rest of my life. At thirty-five, I didn't have a clue about what was next.

19

It Shouldn't Happen to a Goalkeeper Coach

It took a while to come to terms with the fact I wouldn't play again, though there would be the odd opportunity to put the old green jersey and gloves back on in the coming years. If I'd been twenty-eight I'd have attempted a comeback, but as I'd been considering retirement anyway, and had a decent insurance policy, I took my doctor's advice. I'd had a great career and nobody would ever be able to take that away, but I had to think about what would be best for my family and having watched from the stands for a month or so before I called time, I was certain I wouldn't miss playing. During that period, I was asked to do a bit of commentary for Piccadilly Radio, when City played at Portsmouth. I was sitting in the press box in the main stand when a few of the travelling supporters spotted me. Then there were hundreds of City fans shifting over towards where I was and they began singing 'England's, England's number one' and chanting my name. It was fantastic and gave me such a lift when I needed it most, but it summed them up; they are in a different league as far as I am concerned. They hadn't forgotten me and it meant a great deal then and still does today.

Brighton had been an experience and while I'd been there I learned a lot about myself. I also realised how much drink was influencing my life, more than at any other club I'd been at. It was while playing for them that, for the only time in my career, I went into a game drunk. There is no excuse for such a lack of professionalism, but it was the laid-back culture at Brighton that made it so easy. On a Friday after training we went to an Italian restaurant in the town and everybody would have a couple of glasses of wine and then go home. But I was too easily swayed and if anyone said, 'Come and have another one, Joe,' I would tag along. Travelling to Watford on one occasion, I got on the coach with two bottles of brandy in my pocket and drank one in my hotel room the night before the game. We were beaten 3–0 by a very good Watford side – managed by Graham Taylor and with the likes of John Barnes in the side – but while I wasn't to blame for any of their goals, it was totally unacceptable. It made me realise how far I'd allowed myself to drift and since I had more time on my hands than ever before, I had to make sure the boozing didn't get out of control.

The surgeon told me I couldn't do anything for twelve months so we decided to stay in Brighton and enjoy the town, the sea and our beautiful home. I'd started a small haulage company in Macclesfield during my later years at City and when my convalescence ended we moved back to Cheshire so I could give the business a real go. It was one of the biggest mistakes of my life; haulage is a line of work in which solid experience is essential and it is no place for a novice. I had to learn the hard way that I was being ripped off by members of my staff, some of whom knew every trick in the book. The problem was, by the time I realised what was going on it was too late and all my money had gone. I just didn't know enough about the haulage game and wasn't aware of the scams. The stress caused made me physically sick for some time thereafter.

I didn't want to go back to the business world and I decided to stick to what I knew best and that meant moving back into football. I'd learned my lessons, paid the price financially and now had to move on. I'd spoken with my old City teammate Dave Watson and he asked me if I wanted to work for a company called XP Parcel Systems, based in Salford. It would tide me over for a while and I could also use what little experience I had gained in haulage to my advantage as XP had been taken over by TNT and were trying to get their road-haulage side of the business off the ground. The only drawback when I went out to try and drum up business was that most of the guys I was dealing with only wanted to talk about my football career. Then, one afternoon around the end of July 1989, I went to my local golf club in Tytherington where a *Manchester Evening News* golf day had recently ended. Mel Machin and Howard Kendall were having a drink at the bar and we got chatting. Mel asked if I'd like to do the goalkeeper coaching for him at Barnsley and I said I'd love to. He then turned to Howard and asked if City would also consider taking me on. Kendall agreed it was a terrific idea. I told them I was about to go away on a family holiday and they asked me to call them when I returned so we could finalise the arrangements.

We went away, with me still employed by XP Parcels, and on my return I got a call from mum, asking if I'd seen the back of the *Evening News*. I said I hadn't and she then told me the headlines were 'Joe Returns to City'. My first thought was that I hadn't told my boss. I went in to see him and he was brilliant about it, saying he was genuinely pleased for me and wished me all the best. I was going to be self-employed from here on in because goalkeeper coaches were something of a new species in football. While a couple of days at Barnsley and City were great, I needed other sessions to supplement my money. The work, however, was flooding in and no sooner had I handed in my notice at XP than Colin Todd asked if I'd come and do some work at Middlesbrough, which I accepted, and then Stockport asked me to do a day.

I worked for Boro on Monday, City on a Tuesday, Stockport on Wednesday and Barnsley on Thursday, but had to shift things around as things progressed and other clubs came into the equation. I'd do a couple of clubs on the same day, and, later on, a typical working week would see me work with Barnsley and Bradford on Monday and then drive to Middlesbrough and stay overnight, training with them on a Tuesday then drive home and do a local club Wednesday morning. It'd be City on a Thursday morning, Chester in the afternoon and then off to Middlesbrough again on Friday. At my peak, I was doing about 1,200 miles a week. I even spread my wings into Scotland: I worked with Celtic and then flew off to Aberdeen for the day. It was tiring, but very rewarding, and I was at Leeds United the season they won the league championship under Howard Wilkinson. Leeds were a massive club and I was made to feel at home from the day I walked in and they also looked after me financially.

If I was down to do a shift, and it was called off or rearranged by the manager, I'd still get paid, but the smaller clubs couldn't do that and I'd lose a day's money. It was hard work but I had no other choice because this was the life I'd chosen. There was no holiday pay or sick pay and when the English season ended I had to pack up for the summer and go and coach in America for eight weeks. I worked at camps in Florida, Minnesota and Toronto and in many other places.

The American work had come through playing for England Veterans in a tournament in Brazil for the Copa Pele in Rio a few years before. Argentina, Uruguay, Italy and Germany took part and because we'd struggled to get a team together we ended up mixing our squad with other home nations and there were the likes of John Robertson, Peter Osgood, Frank Worthington and Peter Bonetti in the team. The only remit was that everyone had to be over thirty-five, which of course I was. I went out there for three weeks, had a whale of a time and was voted player of the tournament. Because I'd been warned about the dangers of injuring my neck again, I hadn't trained for several years and had put on three stones, but it didn't stop me flinging myself around like an eighteen-year-old. I'd had no repercussions with my neck, which was a huge relief because I was taking a risk playing. The crowds were huge and it went out live on Brazilian television. We returned a couple of years later to play another tournament in Miami and landed the day the Gulf War started. One evening, while I was in a bar watching images of Baghdad being bombed, I got chatting with Pele's agent, Professor Mozay, whom I'd known from my days in the NASL. He asked what I was up to and suggested I should coach in America and he gave me the numbers of people worth talking to. By the time I'd returned home, I'd had an offer of work in Connecticut and that in turn led to my own coaching clinic in Toronto.

I had some adventures, met some characters and had some disappointments, but it was exciting to have what was effectively a new career. Coaching badges weren't a necessity at that time, but I was taking my A badge at Lilleshall national sports centre when I learned I'd been sacked by City. Howard Kendall had left Maine Road and Peter Reid had taken over with Sam Ellis as his right-hand man. All had been well when I'd left at the end of the season and I fully expected to resume at Platt Lane in July, but I think a conversation I had at Middlesbrough probably ended up being my downfall with City. I'd been chatting with Colin Todd and Jim Smith, who'd been sacked by Newcastle, but was lined up for Portsmouth. Jim was doing a few bits and bobs for Colin to tide him over.

Colin asked me how things were at City and I told him I'd overheard a couple of the City players complaining about Sam Ellis's coaching and I knew the fans weren't overjoyed, either. That was all I said, but what I didn't know was that Jim Smith was a big mate of Sam's and I can only assume he told him what I'd said, which hadn't been malicious gossip, just an honest answer to a question. I can't be certain it was Jim who told Sam, but I have my suspicions.

It was a real shame because I loved my time at City. Just going into Platt Lane again as an employee of Manchester City was a great thrill and the first time I arrived back it felt like returning home. I had paid a visit when Billy McNeill had been manager about four years before, just to see a few of the lads. I was standing on the corner watching them train and Alex Williams, who'd just finished a shooting session, shouted hello and I smiled and waved back. McNeill saw this and shouted to Alex: 'Fucking concentrate on what you're doing – he's finished now.' I realised he just wanted to get on with training but he could have been more polite. I was gutted that Billy could show me such a lack of consideration and any respect I'd had for the man evaporated.

As City's keeper coach, however, it had been like old times and a lot of the punters who used to watch me as a player came along to watch the training. I had a great laugh with some of the older blokes, whom I'd known for years. I really was on top of the world. I worked with Tony Coton, Andy Dibble and Martyn Margetson during that period; they were all good lads and worked really hard. I thought Martyn was treated badly by Peter Reid: on one occasion he substituted him at half-time when he was having a bad game. I didn't think that was right and I don't think Martyn ever recovered from the disappointment.

Work was plentiful and I had to go with the clubs that offered most money because I had mouths to feed but, whether it was little Chester or giant Celtic, I loved every minute. Harry McNally, Chester's boss, was a terrific character who loved a drink. He was a very knowledgeable man and a lovely guy, but my abiding memory of him was a fight he had with Keith Bertschin in a wine bar. It was a surreal sight to everybody who witnessed it, with mullets and glasses flying everywhere. During my coaching at Stockport, manager Jimmy Melia asked me to go in goals during one of his eleven-a-side training matches. I did okay and after-wards he asked if I'd be interested in playing again. I asked him in what capacity and he replied, 'To sign as a player.' I was flattered, but told him I didn't think Stockport could afford me. Jimmy said he could sort the wages out but I explained that wasn't the issue. For me to play County would have to cough up the pay-out from the insurance policy. He told me not to worry until I told him how much it was and he nearly fell off his seat. I was forty-one at this point, and it would have been an incredible comeback, but I don't think it would have worked out. I could have done a job, but it just wasn't financially viable.

It was around this time that I watched the 1990 World Cup and despite all that had happened to me since my last involvement with England in 1982, my old mate Peter Shilton was still in goal for the national team. It was great to see him still playing at the highest level but I wasn't sure he was being picked for the right reasons. Was it because he was the outstanding candidate or because people were willing him to break the record for most England caps? He was coming off in some games with twenty minutes to go and he clearly wasn't the keeper he'd been in 1982. The problem was there was no obvious successor: Gary Bailey and Chris Woods never looked like top-class international keepers, not that they were given decent runs to prove themselves.

Nearly all the managers I worked with during my freelance days let me get on with my job. Chris Kamara and Frank Stapleton at Bradford were like chalk and cheese but both were great lads. Howard Wilkinson was very direct and told me exactly how many minutes I had to work with each keeper. At Celtic I worked under Liam Brady and coached Packy Bonner, Brad Friedel and a young Shay Given. Brad couldn't get a work permit, which was a shame, and I told Liam to snap him up if he ever got the opportunity because he was top notch. If Shay had been an inch or two taller, I think he'd have been one of the best in the world; he was an outstanding youngster and it hasn't surprised me how well he's done. John King at Tranmere was a great man and I really enjoyed my time with Middlesbrough, a superbly run club, and I ended up working three days a week for them. Then when Bryan Robson took over he asked if I wanted the job on a full-time basis.

I was delighted to get the offer from Bryan; the only problem was that Liverpool had also indicated they wanted me to continue coaching their keepers on a part-time basis. Graeme Souness had been manager at Liverpool when I started there in October 1993 but he lost his job and

I spoke with Val about the possibility of accepting Robson's offer. I could work for both clubs but the travelling was killing me. I told Boro I would give them an answer the following week because I needed to tell Liverpool what my plans were. Roy Evans had taken over at Anfield by this point and I told him that I was going to accept Middlesbrough's offer. He said, 'No, no – we want you to stay here.' He then rang club secretary Peter Robinson and said he wanted me to be given a full-time job as Liverpool goalkeeper coach. Robinson agreed. With Liverpool only thirty-five miles away, it would have been foolish not to accept their offer, despite the respect I had for Middlesbrough. Obviously my affinity with Liverpool helped swing it, and of course they were one of the biggest clubs in the world. There would be no more travelling up and down motorways, no overnight stays away from the family and no more hairy flights to Aberdeen in a twin-prop aircraft, trying to land with a galeforce wind blowing in from the sea. All the buzzing around had affected my health, primarily because it was so stressful getting to so many different clubs on time.

I couldn't wait to get started at Anfield.

20

This is Anfield

Five days a week and working on match days – that was my new job spec at Liverpool. I was a little mystified as to why I wouldn't be doing any coaching on the day of the game and instead would only attend with a watching brief. I didn't travel to away games, either. This rather hands-off approach to match days must have been a source of frustration for Roy Evans because one day he came in and said, 'We've got to do something about this, Joe.' It was still, in essence, the old Liverpool structure that was in place; it was tried and tested with a belief that, if it wasn't broken, don't fix it. In many ways it was an unusual club to work for because of the rules and regulations you had to abide by. For instance, just because I'd become a full-time member of staff didn't mean I got a company car; it wasn't club policy. Nor was there a mileage allowance and Liverpool argued it wasn't their fault if you chose to live outside the city. It was hard to understand as an outsider, as I was then, because they were one of the biggest clubs in the world yet even Stockport County covered my petrol costs. But I learned that running a tight ship was the Liverpool way and, of course, you couldn't argue that it wasn't extremely successful.

While my professional life was back on track, joining Liverpool coincided with one of the most traumatic periods in my personal life. My mum had just been diagnosed with Alzheimer's disease and my dad was diagnosed with stomach cancer shortly after that. Because of this, mum was moved to hospital as dad had to undergo surgery to remove the tumour, but it was too far gone and we were told that the cancer was terminal. The truth was that dad had sacrificed his health to take care of mum. He had always suffered with stomach ulcers but because of his refusal to let others look after mum, he did everything on his own and it wasn't until later that we found out how much he had put himself through: not eating properly, having to stay awake most of the night as mum would try to get out of the house, and, on the rare occasions she did, he would walk all over town looking for her.

We tried to help dad get away for a short break, but unfortunately he couldn't go because his operation came through so quickly and he was unable to go anywhere. Watching him deteriorate over the next few months was devastating and he eventually passed away in April 1994. It was awful and just before he died he said to me that he wouldn't let a dog suffer the pain he was going through. It was so sad to see a very proud, giant of a man – who taught me so much about life and helped me make the decision to become a professional footballer – fade away to little more than a skeleton.

Mum eventually had to go into a nursing home because of her Alzheimer's and again we had to watch helplessly as the condition took hold and ravaged her body. I remember going to visit her and being told that she had gone to have her hair done. It had been two weeks since I had seen her as I had been in America doing some coaching. I expected to see the jovial, plump woman that was my mum walk into the room. Instead I found myself looking at someone who had had all her bodily fluids removed; her skin, instead of being rosy and clear, was a yellowy-grey colour, stuck on to a skeleton. It was a terrible shock, but we were told by her carers that this was one of the effects of a condition that strips sufferers of their dignity and basic health.

She stayed in the nursing home until she died. I remember I was coming home from Singapore after doing a goalkeeping seminar for FIFA. Val had travelled out to have a holiday in Kho Samui in Thailand, but because she had taken a different flight, she flew back two days before me. We tried to juggle things around so as we could travel together, but there was no way it could be done, so Val went home alone. On my departure, I went to the British Airways desk in Singapore airport and asked for a seat with extra legroom, but was told that because the plane's journey had started in Melbourne, Australia all those seats had been taken. Unbeknown to me a friend of mine, Bill Delahunty, who was a chief steward for BA, knew I was in Singapore and had asked his mate, who was a steward on my flight, if I could be upgraded and as I boarded the plane, I was offered a seat in first class. On landing in Manchester after a wonderfully relaxing flight, Val was there to meet me. As soon as I saw her I knew there was something terribly wrong. She told me that that mum had died during the night. I immediately thought that after what had happened to me on the flight, she was looking after me on my journey home. I still miss them both, and could never thank them enough for all the sacrifices they made to give us the best start in life.

I had to get on with my life as I still had a family to feed and a job to do. My role at Anfield didn't give me too much time to dwell on what had happened and I threw myself into my work and settled in very quickly. We went to Wembley in my first season at the club, playing Bolton in the 1995 League Cup final. But it was amazing to go to such a high-profile game and not be involved in coaching on the day of the game. It seemed like a waste of my knowledge. After all, I'd played at Wembley on several occasions for City and England, and I could have passed on my experience a couple of hours beforehand rather than telling the lads what to expect in the surrounds of Liverpool's Melwood training complex. But if that's what the club wanted, fine by me; they were paying my wages.

A lot of the old boot-room boys were still at the club back then: the likes of Ronnie Moran, Doug Livermore and of course Roy Evans, who had been at Anfield for many years. Sammy Lee had also returned to his spiritual home as reserve-team manager and you could see they looked after their own, which I liked, particularly after some of the experiences I'd had towards the end of my career. They had quite a squad, too. John Barnes, Steve McManaman, Robbie Fowler and Neil Ruddock were among the big names, certainly a lively group of lads. When I'd previously been at the club, on a part-time basis, I had worked with Bruce Grobbelaar, David James and Tony Warner. I think Bruce realised he had one hell of a challenger for his number-one spot in James, who had been keen to work with a specialist goalkeeping coach prior to my arrival. Before that, former QPR goalkeeper Mike Kelly had taken the keepers, but he was Roy Hodgson's assistant for the Switzerland national team and he gave up his role at Anfield because of the time constraints.

The training regime amazed me, too, because after a few stretches, some sprinting and general warm-up exercises it was onto five-a-side football; that's all they ever did. They played with different rules in different games, but it was clear that was a result of years of sticking to what had made the club so successful. It was institutionalised training and as I've always thought that football is a simple game ruined by footballers and managers, I liked the simple approach.

In my second season at Anfield the club again made it to Wembley, this time for an FA Cup-final clash with Manchester United. The one thing people remember about that day is those bloody white suits the players wore. They had been dubbed the Spice Boys and a few of the team bought into it. I would love to know what the great Bill Shankly would have said about it. The lads had decided, off their own bats, to wear the Armani crushed-linen suits and it had been approved by the manager and chairman. But it wasn't just the players who had to wear them, all the staff did too; and yes, that meant one for me. If that brings a smile to your face as you try to envisage me squeezing into one, I don't blame you. Only Ronnie Moran swam against the tide by refusing to wear white and he donned a blue suit instead; but then, he was old school. I weighed about nineteen stones at the time, and, when I first tried my suit on, I looked in the mirror and thought I looked like a sight screen at Lord's cricket ground. I looked huge, and even though the youngsters looked quite smart in theirs, I think it was wrong to ask the rest of us to wear them.

On their day, that Liverpool side were something special, particularly going forward, but they always looked susceptible at the back and we lost the final 1–0 to United. Still, it was an exciting era for the club and the supporters and a great experience for me to be part of it all.

As time went on the players seemed to be having more and more influence on how the club was being run, at least on the playing side, and there would be times I witnessed the likes of John Barnes having animated arguments with Roy Evans and Dougie Livermore in the car park, usually when things weren't going well. The players would sometimes have meetings on their own, with the coaches having to wait outside until they'd finished, something I'd never come across before. I think that hit the likes of Ronnie Moran hard, especially after he'd been at Anfield for so many years and had seen greats like Shankly and Bob Paisley run the club in their image, rather than that of the players.

Before I went full time, one thing I did do on match days was to take part in a half-time penalty competition with supporters. I used to come down the side of the Kop to get on to the pitch and the first time I did it, as one, they started singing 'Who ate all the pies?' as I walked past. They'd never forgotten that incident with the pie from my City days, and although I was well overweight at the time, it was taken in good heart.

We were in Europe every year and though the discipline wasn't all that it should have been, the club were doing okay – and okay by Liverpool standards means very good to the majority of other clubs. Things were far from perfect, though. You'd see players on their mobiles five minutes before training and also before matches, which I didn't feel was right because they should have been concentrating on their jobs. It was also around this time I saw a different side to David James. Jamo should have been the best goalkeeper this country has ever produced, and I don't say that lightly. He had phenomenal agility, great athleticism, a great pair of hands, tremendous reflexes and one of the best physiques I've ever seen on a player. In fact someone once said that if you fed the physical attributes required of a perfect goalkeeper into a computer it would instantly spit out 'David James' as the solution.

In my view his one flaw was lack of concentration and that held him back then, and would continue to dog him throughout his career. It let him down so many times and there was one occasion when he was responsible for a goal that helped Manchester United win at Anfield; the one thing Liverpool fans cannot accept. It seemed to me that Jamo wanted to do things in a flash and would be thinking of the next one before he'd completed the job in hand. On this occasion, he let Paul Scholes score a goal that a goalkeeper with half his talent, but better powers of concentration, would have saved comfortably. I always thought the worst scenario for Liverpool was Jamo having nothing to do for most of the game, because he'd do something silly like racing out of his box when there was no need or chasing a cross that wasn't his to win. It was a side of his game that constantly let him down.

One of the things that hurt me the most was when both David and I had moved to other clubs and he came on as a substitute for England in Copenhagen and had a bit of a nightmare. Later he claimed he hadn't prepared himself mentally to play and that was a hammer blow to me because he'd been a reserve-team keeper when I first started at Liverpool and he ended up playing for England while I was there. I thought that I'd done everything I could to develop him as a player. In my opinion, what he said after the Denmark defeat showed a complete lack of respect for his position and the people he worked for and had worked with.

He was a hard worker but I felt things had to be right for him before he performed to his undoubted potential. He wanted to kick the ball as high as possible and I remember a game against Spurs at White Hart Lane, which had two huge electronic screens at the top of the stands. I went out on to the pitch with a bag of balls but all he wanted to do was to hit the screens with a ball and that too, in my opinion, was indicative of a lack of concentration. He once said that his love for PlayStation games was affecting his focus and I saw it for myself one evening prior to a game at Derby. Roy Evans and Doug Livermore had gone out scouting for the evening leaving Sammy Lee, Ronnie Moran and myself in charge of the lads. The hotel staff had been told to contact us if there were any problems and as it turned out, there were. Room service had knocked on one of the lads' rooms a couple of times to retrieve a trolley but had been told to go away so they asked me if I'd go up and try. I went up with a hotel employee to see if I could help and it turned out to be Dave James's room. He let me in and said he'd been trying to concentrate on PlayStation so it wasn't a surprise to me when he blamed some mistakes on what had obviously become almost an obsession. It surprised me in some ways because he was such an articulate man, very intelligent and a gifted artist. But he had this one chink in his armour that led to the nickname 'Calamity James', which I think will stay with him throughout his career. To my way of thinking had his mind been totally focused on football over the years, he would have been England's number one for more than a decade without any serious challenge.

I enjoyed the European trips with Liverpool and one game that stays in my mind because of the oddness of the place was away to Russian side Vladikavkaz during season 1995/96. It was around fifty miles from the Chechen border and we landed at a military airfield after a terrifying journey on an old Aeroflot plane, which was so old and rickety I half expected to find a bible instead of an in-flight brochure. We were escorted to our hotel under armed guard in the middle of a town that seemed to be stuck in a 1950s time warp. As we arrived at our destination, a Liverpool official jumped on our coach and warned us that at least one English tabloid was trying to set us up and had planted prostitutes in the hotel – so we had to be on our guard from the minute we arrived to the minute we left.

The rooms were disgusting with cockroaches everywhere, even in the fridge. It was frightening. Nevertheless, we won the game 2–1 and as we got on the coach and were about to leave a woman from the hotel came on and said there was a problem. She claimed several towels had gone missing and we'd have to pay for them. Judging by the decrepit rag that had been in my room, I assumed this was a crude attempt to get more money out of the club because most of our lads were millionaires and had no need to pinch anything, let alone a threadbare towel from Cockroach Towers.

We weren't allowed to go without forking out so a token payment was made; a small price to pay to be finally on our way. On landing back at Liverpool, I heard the ground crew were in a state of disbelief at the shocking condition of the Aeroflot's tyres, which were down to the wire mesh. The crew had to fly home with the plane in a precarious state, to say the least, and I recall saying a little prayer for a safe return journey. After that, the club began to hire its own planes for away trips. We reached the quarter-final of the UEFA Cup, but were well beaten by Paris St Germain and I think that was the beginning of the end for Roy Evans because not long afterwards the club announced that Gerard Houllier was going to be joint manager for the 1998/99 campaign. Liverpool had always enjoyed success in Europe but it had been several years since their last triumph. They wanted a man with a track record in European football and Gerard fitted the bill, though the idea of him being joint manager with Roy was doomed to failure. There was also a new and un-wanted job for me. When we began pre-season in Norway and Holland Sammy Lee and I had to sort the kit out for the tour because Ronnie Moran had retired. We were still coaching during the day and now we had an additional job of filling up the skips at Anfield ready for the trip abroad. Because of all the paraphernalia that went with each player's kit, we were still there past eleven at night sorting everything out, which was a new and unpleasant experience.

While in Norway, we had a meeting with Gerard. He had brought in Patrice Bergues as his right-hand man, while Roy and Doug operated as a separate entity. I was still on the coaching staff along with Sammy and

Steve Heighway, who was in charge of the youths. It was an odd set-up because nobody knew who to address as the boss and we'd have briefings from both managers. It was soon clear that it couldn't go on for any length of time. Everyone was trying to walk a fine line, not wanting to upset either side yet unsure who to approach with any queries. Sammy and I had to speak with Gerard about the extra kit duties and he said that it couldn't go on because we were coaches, not kit men, and he quickly sorted out a new guy.

Things were changing and while Roy favoured the tried-and-tested coaching methods, Gerard was a very experienced man and had spent ten years coaching as part of the World Cup-winning France team, developing a group of young players who went on to be very successful. He wanted to concentrate more on the technical side of the game and to bring in more modern training schedules. It was the clash of two worlds, old and new, and eventually, in November 1998, Roy left Anfield after forty years at the club. It was sad to see him go because he was a dyed-in-the-wool Red and a great bloke to work for, but his moving on had been inevitable from the day the club announced Gerard's arrival. Doug Livermore went as well, and, at a meeting shortly afterwards, Sammy Lee was given more responsibility as a first-team coach. I was given the job of managing the reserves as well as being the goalkeeper coach. It was my first role in management and I really enjoyed it. Gerard insisted that the entire coaching staff attended reserve matches because he saw the players at that level as our future. We were bringing youngsters through, keeping fringe players fit, and, if there was an international break, senior players would play to keep their fitness levels high. Gerard also reorganised the physio and medical staff, bringing in specialists who were of great benefit to the club. In addition his assistant Patrice Bergues had a wealth of knowledge and was one of the nicest blokes I ever met in football.

Gerard was quiet, but thorough, and the team he built was excellent. In my second year as reserve-team manager we won the inaugural Barclays Premiership reserve league, which was pleasing from a personal point of view. Gerard made significant changes in a relatively short period of time, bringing in a lot of foreign stars, while disbanding the so-called Spice Boys. He rid the club of its drinking culture, which had been so problematic. I was given the job of enforcing any fines imposed on the squad, which hadn't really existed prior to Gerard's arrival, and had been dealt with in a more in-house way involving senior club officials. On one occasion, Robbie Fowler missed training and Gerard fined him £5,000 and he told him he'd have to either pay it in cash or lose two weeks' wages. Robbie came in to my office, threw £1,000 at me and said, 'Here's your money.' I told him to pick it up, which he did, because it was unacceptable and he paid the remaining £4,000 the day after. Stan Collymore was forever turning up late or occasionally missing training, claiming his mother wasn't well or similar, and there were numerous occasions when his car flew past me on the M62 as he tried to get to Melwood on time. I think it was more down to his unreliability than anything else. Stan wasted his talent: he had it all; pace, power and two good feet but he couldn't handle playing at the highest level. It happens sometimes and it's a shame when you see a kid throwing away his future but, as for mine, I still had one unforgettable season at Anfield to come and I'll treasure the memories of it for as long as I live.

21

One Year ... Five Trophies

Perhaps all those years of having a wonderful affinity with the Liverpool fans had merely been fate clearing a path for me to work at Anfield. There had been the pie incident, the bottle incident, the transfer inquiry. There was also the fact I'd been on the end of so many thrashings that perhaps someone was trying to tell me that, if you can't beat them, join them.

I would spend a decade at Anfield, all told, but the 2000/01 season was nothing short of incredible and to be an active member of the back-room staff for that campaign was very satisfying. We were going well in all cup competitions, both domestically and in Europe, and while we were never going to threaten the Premiership leaders, there was every chance we would win at least one trophy. Phil Thompson was doing a great job as assistant manager to Gerard, whose calm exterior masked a tough disciplinarian core. If you crossed him, you'd know about it. He wouldn't accept a player who didn't want to play or said that he had a slight knock. He wasn't going to carry any passengers and if he had his doubts about the validity of an injury he'd order the player to report twice a day for treatment or send them abroad to receive help. Phil was an excellent addition to his coaching staff not only because was he a Liverpool legend and had a connection to the past but also because he was good at his job.

The European run had left me short of experienced players for the reserves because our games would be on a Thursday night and if the first-team squad had been playing a day or so before in the UEFA Cup, there was no way they'd be asked to play for the second string so soon after. It was getting harder and harder to put out a good side but we plugged away and brought some promising youngsters through.

David James had gone by this point and Brad Friedel had moved on to Blackburn. I felt sorry for Brad because he was a top-notch keeper and I'd been involved in bringing him to Liverpool after being sent to watch him play in America. I knew him from his brief stay at Celtic and rated him back then so the trip to see him play several years later was simply to confirm what I already knew. It took an age to bring him to Anfield due to work-permit problems, but he made it eventually. However, he never really got a break at Liverpool, simply because of the red tape, and ironically the season he left the rule was changed. It was satisfying to see him go on to be one of the best Premiership keepers of recent times. Sander Westerveld came in and did well and I thought he was a good keeper to replace Brad with. In his first season he made a penalty-shoot-out save in the League Cup final against Birmingham City that won us the game, which obviously endeared him to the Liverpool fans.

Robbie Fowler was still hanging on at that point, but he always seemed to be swimming against the tide with Gerard's style of management. He occasionally celebrated goals in a manner that Gerard didn't like (think Everton, chalk lines and sniffing) and I think he knew his days were numbered at Anfield, despite his tag of 'God' on the Kop. Yet even after these incidents Gerard was still loyal to Robbie in public. Gerard had a few training ground spats that suggested all wasn't well and the 2000/01 season would be his last at the club, though, in fairness, it was quite a swansong. We went on to win the FA Cup against Arsenal, where we were well outplayed on the day but managed to nick it through Michael Owen's two goals, and some of Sander's saves in that game were outstanding. Then, four days later, we had the UEFA Cup final to look forward to. We played Spanish side Alaves at the Westfalenstadion, Dortmund and flew out of the blocks, leading two–nil after just sixteen minutes. Then their coach, José Manuel Esnal, made a tactical switch that brought them right back into the game. Although we went 3–1 up, they pulled it back to 3–3 before Robbie scored what looked like the winner, only for Jordi Cruyff to level in the last minute. This was the

first final to be settled by a golden goal – and
effect it was a golden own goal just four minutes
one of the most incredible games I've ever witnessed.
Premiership game to play so the celebrations were very
was amazed by the number of people who had travelled from
we must have had 40,000 fans there that night.

In that final league game we beat Charlton to finish third
clinched a slot in the Champions League. Robbie was back to his best
scoring a hat-trick, though he'd move on to Leeds not long after. Three
trophies and a Champions League spot – it was an amazing season and
fully endorsed the new methods Gerard had introduced. The million or
so fans that turned out to welcome us home on an open-top bus tour of
the city render mere words and descriptions pointless, such was the
emotion and excitement that day. You had to be there and I was still
pinching myself that I was part of it.

It was announced shortly after that Patrice Bergues had to leave due
to family reasons and it put a real dampener on the celebrations. Patrice
had been a key part of a fantastic backroom staff that had become a
family and would be a major loss to the club and the people who had
been fortunate enough to work with him. Gerard brought in Jacques
Corvelsier, a coach he knew from his days in France, but he didn't have
the same impact as Patrice, and in consequence more of the coaching
workload was put onto the shoulders of Sammy and Phil. It did however
gave Sammy a chance to step up to the plate and I think he did an excellent job and never really received the credit he deserved. Perhaps he will
prosper now he's been taken on as first-team coach at Anfield once again;
I really hope so because I think he deserves a bit of luck following his
spell as Bolton manager. Sammy had nurtured Michael Owen and Jamie
Carragher, who both went straight into his reserve team rather than to
the academy because they were both phenomenal talents. In my view
Sammy did more than anyone to help them make the transition from
promising kids to outstanding first-team players.

Steve Gerrard had been part of the academy but had really been
struggling with his fitness due to an imbalance in his spine and hips,
and, despite his incredible ability, there were concerns about whether
he'd be able to progress or not. He was a tall, gangly lad who was head
and shoulders above his peers, but the physical problems weren't going

we scored it, though in
from the end. It was
We still had one
low key but I
Liverpool;
and

see how good he actually was.
inst Leeds United, along with
after the game Sammy and I had
e had a meeting with the gaffer
he two kids who had played and
only problem was that he couldn't
because he was in too much pain.
ng players, he reckoned he could
t of the academy and base him at
l supervision and a strengthening
hysios. Fortunately for Liverpool,
it worked a ...., ngth to strength and much of the credit for that has to go to Gerard Houllier.

Losing Patrice seemed to put extra strain on Gerard, who was a hard-working manager anyway, and although Phil Thompson shouldered his fair share of the workload, Gerard was piling the pressure upon himself. We'd started the 2001/02 season by adding the Charity Shield and the Super Cup to become the first English club to win five trophies in one calendar year and were going well in the league. It would be nearly impossible to emulate that kind of success, but Gerard was doing all in his power to do just that. We didn't know how badly it was affecting his health until we played Leeds United at Anfield. The match reached half-time and he gave his usual team talk and then Sammy and Phil gave individual players more specific instructions. Gerard walked past me clutching his chest and asked me where the club doctor, Mark Waller, was. I told him he was in his room as usual and he left to see him. I could see he wasn't well and told Phil as much. I went down to the doctor's room and he was examining Gerard. He said Phil would have to take over because Gerard was going to hospital. It was a shock because nobody knew just how serious his condition was. It transpired he would need an aorta dissection to save his life because, without prompt action, he could have died within hours.

I had to go and find his wife, Isabelle, and told her Gerard was ill and I then took her to the doctor's room before updating Phil Thompson. Gerard had his operation later that evening and the surgeons had warned Isabelle that it was touch and go because of the nature of his heart problem. Thankfully, it was a success and he not only recovered but also went on to show what a tough character he was by returning to Anfield and later becoming manager at Lyon.

The odd thing about the whole episode was that had it happened before the game, or in its aftermath, he would have died, but, because it was half-time, we had a doctor on hand and there were no crowds outside to delay the ambulance so he got to hospital in the nick of time. We flew to Russia the next day and if it had happened on the plane he'd have had no chance. The club doctor had stayed with him after he'd been admitted and because he was there and noticed his blood pressure had dropped, he raised the alarm and he was transferred to Broad Green.

He returned to France to convalesce but there was no way he was going to give up football. In fact he would call the coaching staff three times a week to discuss things and get an update on the work at Melwood, which he had overseen, and was now one of the best training complexes in the country. Phil and Sammy were brilliant and steadied the ship in his absence, which lasted five months all told before he turned up, unannounced, prior to a game against Borussia Dortmund, which we had to win to qualify for the knockout stages of the Champions League. It gave everyone a tremendous lift, though he explained he was there just to listen and watch, not actively take part. Nevertheless we won 2–0, with Steven Wright scoring the second goal. He returned to work shortly after that, but, by his own admission, it was too soon and he took charge of the Champions League quarter-final second leg at Bayer Leverkusen. His decision to take off the influential Didi Hamann, with the score at 1–1 and Liverpool leading on aggregate, backfired badly. We lost 3–1 and missed the chance of meeting Manchester United in the semi-final.

My final year at Anfield was horrible. Watching Gerard try to prove that his health was good by working even harder was a difficult experience. I'd relinquished control of the reserves because it was affecting my job as a goalkeeper coach. There was an element of player power starting to emerge once again and it was obvious that all was not well. Our tried-and-tested routine in Europe of playing the away leg, stopping over afterwards and then flying home the next day was questioned by some players, who arranged a meeting with Gerard to voice their concerns, which would have never happened before. Players had always done what they were told when they were told during Gerard's reign, but there was a definite resistance to some of his methods in the 2003/04 season and

Gerard himself became less approachable as a manager, purely because of the enormous pressure he was under. The Champions League became an obsession at the club and at one meeting I heard that Gerard was told that qualification for next season's competition was the very least that was required if he was to keep his job. After a defeat to Marseilles in the UEFA Cup, the writing was on the wall for him and on 24 May 2004 Gerard Houllier vacated the manager's office at Anfield and was replaced by Rafa Benitez. The new manager, as new managers often do, wanted to bring in his own backroom staff and I sensed there was no place for me any more, so I decided to leave Anfield for pastures new. It had been a wonderful decade at a wonderful club but all good things must come to an end.

I was desperate to stay in football and so I contacted Ray Clemence who invited me to do some keeper coaching for the England under-eighteen side. Sammy McIlroy asked if I'd like to do a bit of coaching at Stockport and Ian Rush, who'd recently taken over at Chester, asked me do a similar job for him. It was all starting again, the coaching merry-go-round, just as it had when I first got into that line of work. I didn't mind because I needed to earn a wage and I particularly enjoyed being involved with England. Nigel Pearson was the under-eighteen manager and on my way home from Slough, where the training camp had been based, I got a call from Billy Stewart, the goalkeeper coach at Liverpool's academy. He told me Steve Heighway had asked whether he'd mind if I came back to do some coaching for the academy. I met Steve and he told me that whatever had happened at the club, the academy was a separate entity and they did things their own way. He added that he didn't want to see a person of my quality go, which was pleasing to hear and appreciated. How could I say no?

I would coach the Liverpool youngsters twice a week and, with my work at Chester and Stockport, things were going better than I'd dared to hope. I loved teaching younger players how to be a goalkeeper because they had no baggage and were there to listen and learn. It was a different concept for me and it felt very fulfilling, but I was about to receive a call that would take me away from the north-west and to the Midlands, where I was about to be offered a chance to work with a club that, like their fantastic supporters, would be going boing-boing over the next few, exhilarating years.

22

Throstle's Nest

In November 2004 Bryan Robson had just taken over as manager at West Bromwich Albion and, out of the blue, Nigel Pearson called to see if I was interested in taking on a part-time role at the Hawthorns. Fred Barber had been the keeper coach up to that point, but he held a similar part-time role at Bolton and Robson, not without good reason, felt it wasn't right for him to be coaching a team that would be in opposition twice a season. He wanted someone else in so he asked me and I was happy to accept.

I started off by doing two days a week plus match days and then, during an international break, we flew out to Florida and Bryan asked if I'd take on the job full time, and I was delighted to accept. It turned out to be an unforgettable first season and though the team were struggling near the bottom of the Premier League, I remember going to play City at the City of Manchester stadium and us not having a single shot or so much as a corner, and yet we somehow managed to draw 1–1 thanks to Richard Dunne scoring a freakish own goal. As he tried to control the ball during one of our attacks the ball bounced off his shin and the pace on it meant the on-rushing David James had no chance. Rob Earnshaw tried to get the final touch but it was already over the line and he ended up like a stranded fish in the back of net. That proved to be the turning point in our season and we suddenly found a belief that we could escape the drop.

Our last-but-one game was against Manchester United at Old Trafford and we were 1–0 down when our goalie Russell Holt had to come off having sustained an injury. Sub goalie Tomasz Kuszczak came on and managed to defy the laws of gravity and logic as he repelled everything United could throw at him. He had a terrific game and we managed to nick a goal and earn an excellent 1–1 draw. It was hard to believe that every other result had gone our way that day. So despite looking doomed prior to kick-off, we now had an outside chance of staying up if everything went our way on the final day of the season, when we were due to face Portsmouth. It would be a nervy, amazing last match and I don't think I've ever been involved in such an emotional rollercoaster of an afternoon in my career – and this from a man who played for Manchester City for seventeen years!

One minute we were staying up, the next we were going down as latest scores were fed to us and, with several clubs around us embroiled in the relegation dogfight, the tension was unbearable. There were so many scenarios and possible permutations that it was going to be impossible to create a clear picture of what was likely to happen. All we knew was we had to do our bit and win our game against Portsmouth and then hope for the best. It was between us Crystal Palace, Norwich and Southampton but if we failed to win, we were down – end of story. Palace were at home to Charlton Athletic who didn't really have anything to play for, Norwich were at Fulham and Southampton were playing at home to Manchester United. With ten minutes gone, Norwich went behind and Southampton took the lead; rumours swept the ground but none of them mattered if we couldn't score ourselves. By the break we were still goalless, Palace were behind, Saints drawing and Norwich were out of it altogether.

We still had a chance and Robbo geed the lads up for one final push at the end of what had been an exhausting season, both mentally and physically. Finally, on fifty-eight minutes, Geoff Horsfield put us 1–0 up, then Southampton fell behind and Palace equalised. As things stood, we were safe – until Palace went 2–1 ahead. It needed something dramatic to happen. Kieran Richardson made it 2–0 for us and with roughly ten minutes to go, our fans went wild as news filtered through that Charlton had made it 2–2. Palace needed to score again and Southampton needed to find two goals – it had tilted our way but there was still time for anything to happen.

The final whistle went in our game and we then had to wait for the outcome at Selhurst Park to see if we'd done enough. Those few minutes seemed to last forever but then the whole place erupted – Palace had drawn 2–2 and they would be going down, not West Brom. It was a tremendous achievement to beat the drop considering we had been in last place at Christmas. In fact I believe we are the only club in Premiership history that has survived after being at the foot of the table over the festive period. I needed a lengthy break after that – we all did – because it wasn't going to be any easier next season.

During the summer of 2005, Chris Kirkland was brought in but suffered yet another setback when he broke his finger. But for his continual setbacks, I believe he would now be England's number on; he is an amazingly talented young man. Tomasz Kuszczak had an incredible season, but despite Robbo's best efforts, we couldn't repeat the previous campaign's heroics and we were eventually relegated at the end of 2005/06. On the back of an impressive year, Kuszczak was offered the chance to join Manchester United for £2.5 million, plus United keeper Luke Steele, while Kirkland went back to Liverpool. In September 2006, Bryan Robson was sacked as Albion boss. Nigel Pearson took over in a caretaker capacity and did very well for the four games he was in charge, before Tony Mowbray was unveiled as the new Albion manager on 13 October 2006. Nigel left shortly after, disappointed, I imagine, not to have had a crack at the job himself and became assistant to Sam Allardyce at Newcastle United.

To his credit, Tony, a very likeable guy, kept all the backroom staff so it was business as usual behind the scenes, though of course he brought in his own ideas. During his first season, we had a number of problems with a goalkeeper called Pascal Zuberbuhler, 'Zubi', who had been brought in prior to Bryan Robson's sacking. Tony decided to keep him as the club's number one and let him prove himself and why not? Zubi was a Switzerland international, an experienced pro and a nice man, but he never seemed to get the rub of the green or win the confidence of the supporters, some of whom, in all fairness, didn't give him much of a chance. It was a shame, but it happens in football and while I could relate to some of the problems he was having from my own experiences as a young pro, after he cost us a couple of goals at home to QPR, Tony decided he needed a player who knew what playing at the top in England was all about.

He signed Dean Kiely from Portsmouth, where he'd recently been relegated to third choice following David James's arrival from Manchester City and the emergence of rookie keeper Jamie Ashdown. Disillusioned with life at Fratton Park, he jumped at the chance to move to the Hawthorns and his experience and ability proved a valuable addition to the team and went a long way to almost winning Albion promotion. We had been flying and then had a blip around February and March when the players became edgy at home due to the expectation levels. Despite this, Tony did a great job steering the side to the play-off final at Wembley, having seen off Wolves in the semi-finals. We'd now face Derby County for the right to once again play Premier League football.

After being denied the chance to coach on the pitch for Liverpool at the old Wembley, I was now going to have the chance to once again kick a ball on that lush, green turf during the warm-up – only this time it was at the new Wembley stadium. It was fabulous to be back, though a bit strange because the last time I'd been out on the pitch in a working capacity had been the 1981 centenary FA Cup final against Spurs, twenty-six years earlier. Being a traditionalist, and despite the stadium being state of the art in every sense, it just wasn't the same special feeling being at Wembley again. The pitch was in exactly the same position, but just like the City of Manchester stadium will never be the same as Maine Road, the new version of Wembley will never be the same as the old one, at least for me. I still can't believe they could integrate the old Twin Towers into the make-up of the stadium – but there you go. I walked back to the spot Ricky Villa had scored the winning goal for Spurs and relived the moment for a few seconds, and then it was back to business helping our keepers prepare for the play-off final.

The game itself was disappointing. Derby County had done their homework and prevented us playing the free-flowing football Tony had instilled in the side throughout the season. It was one of the rare occasions we didn't score, and despite Kevin Phillips going close, Derby won 1–0. I felt we were the better side, but they edged it, though by their own admission they weren't prepared for life at the top and endured a miserable campaign during 2007/08. The gap between the divisions is huge and if you're not ready and don't have the right experience on board, you'll get swallowed up.

Disappointed though everyone was in the dressing room after the game, Tony said, 'That's it. You have to draw on your strengths and learn from the mistakes we've all made this season and come back stronger next season.' The lads absorbed those words, and though we would lose a number of them in the close season, to their credit that's exactly what they did.

Jason Koumas, Diomansy Kamara and Curtis Davies all went for big money and Tony brought in players like Ishmael Miller from Manchester City and Roman Bednar from Hearts while holding on to the talents of players like Kevin Phillips, Robert Koren and Zoltan Gera. We started steadily without tearing trees up as the team gelled. But we were scoring goals for fun, although conceding a fair few too. Set pieces became our Achilles heel and it was a big problem for us all season. The football was great and the games never less than entertaining, but 3–2 score lines were far more common than 1–0 victories. Concentrating too much on our defensive weaknesses, in Tony's opinion, might have taken something away from our free-flowing, attacking football and he was reluctant to change the way the team played, with good reason. As long as we scored one more than our opponents, we'd be fine and few doubted we were the best football team in the division, but what a hard campaign it turned out to be.

I thought the 2006/07 season had been tough, but I don't think there's ever been a season like 2007/08, with the financial rewards greater than ever before and everyone, from top to bottom, wanting a piece of it. It was so difficult, at times it was like a keenly contested horse race, with everyone tightly packed in but nobody wanting to take the lead and to pull away. It was incredible, but, to Tony's credit, he never wavered from his belief in attractive, attacking football. He stuck to his guns and as the season wore on, we were well placed to strike for home, always on the shoulders of the leaders without moving past them.

We were also having a great run in the FA Cup, which was throwing up a high number of shocks. We made it to the semi-final, which meant another return to Wembley, but for me, that's a game that should be played on a neutral club ground because it takes the prestige away from reaching the final – the only game I believe should be played there. I understand why the FA plays the semis there because it gives a lot more people the chance to have an unforgettable day out, but I still don't agree with it.

We were fourth in the league with a handful of games left and facing

Portsmouth in the semis for a chance of an FA Cup final. Had we won that game, I'm not sure what effect it would have had on us, but I felt losing the game was the turning point in our season. Tony refocused the lads and we had a vital game at Blackpool a few days later so we didn't have time to dwell on our defeat. We travelled to Bloomfield Road, perhaps still with a few cobwebs to blow away, and fell behind to a set-piece goal. Then Dean Kiely made an incredible save about ten minutes later – from another set-piece – and the lads battled through to the eighty-first minute when substitute Kevin Phillips equalised from the spot. From then on, there was only one team in it and Phillips and Miller scored again as we won 3–1 to go back to the top of the Championship for the first time in two months. Our away form from then on was superb, and although we still had a few odd results at home – a 4–1 defeat to Leicester among them – we knew that a point against Southampton in our penultimate game of the season would take us up.

Of course, Saints were by that time being managed by Nigel Pearson, and they led 1–0 until the last few seconds when Chris Brunt equalised to all-but guarantee promotion thanks to a vastly superior goal difference. We then went to QPR, backed by a fantastic away support, all in fancy dress as has become the tradition at Albion for the last game, and were crowned champions after a 2–0 win. It was a great end to a breath-taking season – now the real hard work will once again begin for Tony, his backroom staff and his players and I'm incredibly happy to be starting my fifth year at The Hawthorns.

23

View from the Sticks

It's been a hell of a journey for me and I do appreciate how fortunate I've been to be involved with football on a professional level for more than forty years. By this point you'll be well aware that the highs have been incredibly high and the lows have been very low. There has never a period in which things just trundled along smoothly and there's been drama at every club I've worked at. Manchester City will always be my first love and I support them as a fan these days, unless the club I'm employed by is playing them, of course. A club like City is impossible to get out of your system, and, in all honesty, I wouldn't want it to be. I would have dearly loved to have gone back and worked for City after that brief stay in 1990, but maybe some things just aren't meant to be.

There have been terrific characters along the way and I've made some fantastic mates in that time, too. I've also lost a few. My old mate Arthur Mann died in tragic circumstances in the mid-Seventies and Kaziu Deyna died in a car crash in America in the late Eighties. Young Tommy Caton was taken long before his time and in more recent years George Heslop passed away, though I'm sad that nobody bothered to pick up the phone and tell me he had died. What his family must have thought of me for missing his funeral, I've no idea. George, my old mate, I would have paid my final respects if I had been allowed to, but you know that, don't you?

To round this book off, I think it's only right to talk about the current state of English goalkeeping and how the conveyor belt of talent has gone from the torrent it was in the Seventies to the trickle of today. I was always fortunate in my career to have had people who helped me push forward to the next level. In Malcolm Allison I had a coach who was twenty years ahead of his time, at least in his first incarnation at City. He brought in Bert Williams, a Wolves and England legend, to work with me long before anyone else thought of goalkeeper coaches. To listen to Bert's advice and have someone like that show you the ropes, was awe inspiring and it gave me a definite edge.

Then I was lucky to speak with Bert Trautmann at a crucial time in my career. Having Bert tell me he'd had worse games than the one I'd just had against West Ham – which we lost 5–1 at Maine Road – was pivotal to my mental development as a goalkeeper. It was around that time that the coaching seed was first planted in my head, because just being able to talk to someone who'd been there, bought the T-shirt and worn it with pride was invaluable. Bill Taylor was a fantastic coach, full of innovative ideas, and I was also lucky to also get to work with my hero, Harry Gregg, for a period of time. Harry was perhaps the biggest influence on my career and I will be forever in his debt. I try to give back what I learned from these great men by coaching other keepers and promising youngsters.

Things have changed, though, and nowadays players like me wouldn't be given the chance to get it right. You have to perform instantly or you might never get another opportunity and that can't be right. That kind of pressure is unfair and counter productive. The period of nurturing needs to be there because snap judgements, more often than not, turn out to be wrong. I should know. Clubs are more willing to shop abroad for a goalie and pay several million to get a quick fix rather than develop a promising youth player and help him mature. It's worth remembering that keepers take until they are twenty-five before they are even close to fulfilling their potential; up to that point, they are still learning their trade. I am still learning new things forty-odd years on. It is frightening what's happening in today's game and I don't think it bodes well for the future.

Look at Ben Foster and Scott Carson, two great prospects, but we only know that because they've gone out on loan to other clubs to prove it. What would have happened if they'd remained in the reserves at Manchester

United and Liverpool? Would they have ever got their chance in the first-team? Probably not. I think the FA has to look at the bigger picture because that trickle of talent might dry up completely. If FIFA does bring in a rule that stipulates a certain proportion of home-grown players have to be included in a starting line-up, I think it can only be beneficial for the game in England.

Though I love my job, I'm not even sure there is a need for top goal-keeping coaches at football clubs. That's because I believe those coaches should be teaching ten-to-fifteen-year-olds; that's when expert advice is really needed. My job is more to keep the keepers I work with ticking over. When I was at Anfield, I got the most enjoyment from coaching English youngsters at under-sixteen, seventeen and eighteen levels at the academy. The kids have to be taught by people who know what playing with the elite is all about, sentiments echoed by Peter Shilton and Ray Clemence. This happens on the Continent, but not in England, which is why so many young keepers at professional clubs in this country seem to be lacking in even the most basic skills and techniques. The gap between clubs in the Premier League and the Championship and beyond is grow-ing all the time, and unless you're being taught by someone who has played in high-pressure situations, how can you be prepared for what might happen at the top level?

For the FA to pay £800 million for a new stadium that might get used ten times a year, but not to have a school of excellence – in which coaches like Ray Clemence, Shilts, myself and others could pass on their experience – is ridiculous. I passionately believe that too many people who have played and worked at the top have been discarded when their input should be utilised. It's not too late to change; we just need to invest experience in our youth at the right time and have patience. It is a blue-print that will bear fruit in years to come. That is surely not unreason-able when you consider the impact it might have on our future interna-tional team and club sides.

As for the kids around now I'd choose Chris Kirkland, Ben Foster, Joe Hart and Scott Carson as the future of English goalkeeping. Hart, in particular, looks set for a terrific future now he is playing first-team football for City. In fact, a few people have pointed out that both Joe and I have trod similar paths: we both played at Shrewsbury Town and then turned out for City as teenagers and he's already won recognition with the full England squad. There's not much more out there, to my knowledge. Paul Robinson's confidence was at rock bottom at the time of writing, though it would be foolish to write him off and a change of club could well solve Robbo's problems. David James's performances over the past few years merited an England recall and all credit to him – and also to Fabio Capello for picking a team based on form rather than just reputation.

Talking about Mr Capello I have to ask, however, why has an Italian keeper coach has been brought in for our national team? It's beyond me. I also think it's a travesty that Ray Clemence has been pushed sideways, though ironically his new role as the FA's head of development means he will work more with the younger players that are coming through; time will tell. Football is changing at such a rapid pace and I wonder how long it will be before there are virtually no English players in the Premier League. I think Capello should maybe go with someone like Joe Hart or Scott Carson, give them a good run in the side and let them bed in properly rather than just making the odd appearance here and there.

We used to be a nation that produced the best goalkeepers in the world, but that's not the case any more. Ask yourself why there are no English keepers playing on the Continent? Expand that question to why are there no top English outfield players playing on the Continent? At the academies of our top clubs, we've got schoolteacher-type coaches looking after kids when it should be the best coaches available. Newcastle United are a perfect example of how a club can throw money down the drain, paying millions to a succession of sacked managers when it could have gone towards developing a fantastic academy with top coaches. I'm not sure where the game is headed but I fear for England as an international side and even if the problems are addressed now, I think it could be ten or fifteen years before we are a major force again.

As things stand, and if I was thirty years younger, I would now be England's outright number one, just as the City fans always claimed I was and I believed myself to be. That's not me being big headed; it is simply my opinion. Things didn't work out that way, of course, but I'm not complaining. I've had a fantastic career and to think it all came about by a quirk of fate. Had I not been spotted playing goal during a half-time knockabout for AEI training school, who knows which direction my life might have taken? As it is, I'm in my fifth decade of employment in professional football and I'm probably physically fitter than I was when I first started out as a teenager. I'm still enjoying the game as much as when I used to throw myself around on that piece of waste ground opposite our house as a kid. For that, I count myself a very privileged man. I couldn't have done any of it without a fantastically supportive family and I thank them all for the sacrifices they made along the way.

There are people and places I'll remember more than others and one thing I'll never forget is the advice Harry Gregg gave me when I was at Shrewsbury. It is advice that every young keeper should heed. In that heavy Northern Irish accent, he told me:

> Joe, you're a nice young kid, but when you cross that line, I want you to become a bastard. You hate being beaten and you hate defenders more than you hate forwards – defenders never listen to you – and you always have to make up for their mistakes but they never make up for yours.

How right he was.

As for my old club Manchester City, I was thrilled when Sven-Goran Eriksson took over. He seemed to be guiding the club in the right direction, taking them to a respectable ninth in the Premiership in 2007/08 after the club had finished in fourteenth place under different management the season before. I was therefore surprised and rather disappointed when he was sacked but it just proves my point that only overnight success is tolerated in the modern game. Nevertheless, I wish Mark Hughes well and I hope he can take City back to their rightful place in English football. With the crowd potential we have there is no reason why a Champions League spot should be beyond us, especially if the signing of Jo is followed by others of a similar calibre. The City fans deserve the best and I'm sure Denis Law was as relieved as anyone when the Blues beat United at Old Trafford in February 2008 to complete a first league double in thirty-eight years. So now, when people hark back to his last league goal, against United in 1974, at least it is no longer the last time City won a game there.

As for me, I hope people think of me as a decent bloke off the pitch, but one who hated getting beaten on it. In the late Sixties, Malcolm Allison used to tell people he was the greatest coach in the world. For a period of time during the Seventies and early Eighties, I was the best goalkeeper in the world. I just didn't shout about it loudly enough. Sometimes, being the best just isn't enough.

24

Dream Team

Before I sign off I would like to present my all-time City side from those I had the privilege of playing with at Maine Road. Due to the length of time I spent at the club – seventeen years – I straddled a number of different teams and played with most of the greats from the late Sixties to the early Eighties. I think that longevity has given me an excellent perspective and I have really enjoyed picking the side. These are the eleven guys I consider the best of the best, plus my five substitutes.

1
Joe Corrigan

2
Tony Book

4
Tommy Booth

5
Dave Watson

3
Glyn Pardoe

6
Mike Summerbee

7
Asa Hartford

8
Colin Bell

10
Neil Young

11
Brian Kidd

9
Francis Lee

Subs: Alex Williams, Alan Oakes, Kaziu Deyna, Joe Royle, Tony Towers

Manager: Joe Mercer

Coach: Malcolm Allison

Formation: 4-4-2

1 Joe Corrigan

Self-explanatory!

2 Tony Book

Given his achievements in the game (which included being named player of the year in 1969, jointly with Dave Mackay) it is incredible to think that Booky only made his debut in senior football at the age of twenty-nine. He was the best captain I played under, for a number of reasons: he was a father figure, a great footballer and knew the game inside out. He enjoyed a cigarette and half a pint of bitter and was always so approachable. I always remember him coming over to me after I'd conceded a goal in the first few minutes of the 1970 League Cup final. He put his arm around my shoulder and just said: 'Come on son, just forget about it, we need to get on with it. It's over and done with now.' That very human touch helped me more than any bollocking could have done and we went on to win the game. He was universally respected – a good, decent man who could have represented England had he played for City five years sooner.

3 Glyn Pardoe

A great player, who was City's youngest ever debutant at the tender age of fifteen. He was also a great bloke, whose career met with a tragic end. Originally a centre forward Glyn was skilful and a great passer of the ball and he should have played for England. He was also versatile; naturally right footed, he adapted easily to his usual role at left back. I recall being in a pre-season training camp with him in Sweden and it must have been one of the hottest summers on record. We were jogging round a pitch and there was a sprinkler on in the centre circle. Glyn started with his training gear on but ended with nothing but his socks and trainers as he kept running to the middle as he passed the sprinkler in order to cool down before rejoining us. He was overweight back then, so to see this naked, little, stout bloke running round like that is something you don't forget – however hard you try!

4 Tommy Booth

If Tommy were playing today, I think he'd be classed as another Alan Hansen. He had superb technical skills for a central defender and in addition was good in the air and highly reliable. He might not have been the quickest but he'd always give you 100 per cent. Tommy is still one of the funniest men I've ever met; I remember when we were kids, we were staying at the Waldorf hotel in London and ordering from an a la carte menu. In my ignorance, I ordered a minute stake – pronouncing minute as in minute meaning 'tiny'. I said to the waiter, 'Can I have a minute steak? In fact, as they are minute, I'll have two.' Tommy fell off his seat laughing and the bugger has never let me forget it to this day.

5 Dave Watson

Dave was great in the air, a fantastic header of the ball. He may not have been the most technically gifted player but he was as tough as teak; a brave defender you could always rely on to throw himself in the way of the ball. It is no surprise to me that he became such a favourite with the fans. Malcolm Allison's decision to sell him in 1979 was one of the many catastrophic errors made at that time. I remember I knocked him out years after he'd left City and gone to Southampton. I'm sure Dave remembers it: I missed the ball and punched him instead as he headed it into the net. After my right hook he was out cold and lying on the ground.

6 Mike Summerbee

What can I say about Mike? He was an exceptional player who was as comfortable on the wing as he was through the middle. But I feel he wasn't given the credit he deserves. He gave as much as he got and was hard as nails. I remember him taking me on in the dressing room at Coventry after a cross I'd dropped led to their winning goal. It was in the heat of the moment and because he was a natural-born winner I fully expected him to take a swing at me. But Booky stepped in to calm things down and it was forgotten ten minutes later. I know Ron 'Chopper' Harris cited Buzzer as one of the hardest opponents he ever faced and that tells you all you need to know. They kicked lumps out of each other but neither backed down. Has there ever been a tougher winger than

Mike Summerbee? He was also a great lad, as this story shows. Just after I signed for City my mum was in a dry cleaner's in Sale Moor when Mike walked in. The woman who worked in the shop told Buzzer that I would be joining him at Maine Road and my mother, who was always looking out for me, asked Mike if he would take care of her little boy. The next morning Mike came into the reserve-team dressing room and asked: 'Is Joe Corrigan here?' The rest of the lads thought I had done something wrong and every eye in the room was focused on me. I slowly stood up and, when Mike saw how tall I was, he just blurted out: 'You should be looking after me. Never mind me looking after you!' Nor will I ever forget Mike sitting on the ball in front of the Kop at Anfield – it infuriated them, but he didn't even bat an eyelid.

7 Asa Hartford

A good passer, quick and as hard as nails, he played in the World Cup finals for Scotland in 1978 and 1982. He could score goals and gave 100 per cent on and off the pitch; that was the Asa Hartford I knew. I loved to be in his company. I recall going out to a supporters' club at Holyhead, Anglesey with Asa and the rest of the team and we stayed in a local hotel. We had a few beers on the bus and also in the hotel bar, and Booky, by then our manager, asked me as club captain to make sure the lads went to bed at a reasonable hour because we had a game at the weekend. But Asa didn't want to turn in. I really had to work hard to convince him, and, later that night, when I was doing the rounds of the players' rooms I knocked on Asa's door and asked if he was okay. 'Yeah, leave me alone you big bastard,' he shouted. I considered going in and teaching him a lesson but decided not to. The next morning Asa told me he hadn't realised the door was still unlocked when he'd said it!

8 Colin Bell

The fittest footballer I ever played with and one of the greatest players I've ever seen. He could run all day and was a dedicated professional but I still don't think people realise just how good he was. He could pass, shoot, head and run; he had it all. I even remember him beating running coach Derek Ibbotson in a canter over 440 yards without even breaking sweat. He won forty-eight caps for England – a record for a City player –

and he would have got even more but for that injury at Old Trafford. A quiet man and a decent bloke.

9 Francis Lee

Franny was a truly great player and a man with bags of self-confidence. Despite his chunky build he had phenomenal speed over five yards and he forced defenders into fouling him, winning a huge amount of penalties in the process. He could strike a ball with ferocious power and scored many memorable goals from outside the box. He was a winner with the heart of a lion, and I believe he was the first City player to take part in the World Cup finals. He stood up for what he believed was right for the team, but, while he'd dish out many a bollocking, he'd be the first to back you up in a crisis. Franny loved champagne and I remember going for lunch one day with Malcolm and meeting Franny and Rodney Marsh at a hotel and drinking champagne all afternoon. Lunch ended about eight in the evening after fourteen bottles of Cristal champagne. He worked hard and played hard, like most lads back then.

10 Neil Young

Bacardi and Coke and a cigarette; my abiding memory of Neil is a little orange light in the darkness on the back of a plane for twenty-six hours on a flight to Australia. And when we landed in Oz he wasn't even drunk! He had a sweet left foot and defined the word elegance both on and off the pitch. One of his many attributes was the ability to swerve a ball with pace, long before lighter footballs were introduced. I think he used his right leg to stand on, but with a left peg like that who could complain. He complemented the forward line perfectly and was a nice bloke, too.

11 Brian Kidd

Kiddo was a fantastic striker who scored freely at every club he played for. He was very left-footed, which defenders realised, but they still couldn't prevent him doing what he did. Although he was an unassuming lad Brian would speak up if he thought something wasn't right and I think it was probably his outspoken nature that led to Malcolm discarding him during his second spell as coach at Maine Road. Leaving City hurt Kiddo and it's a pity he didn't stay at the club longer. I am also convinced that his prowess as a coach helped Manchester United become the force they are today, even if it pains me to say it!

Subs:

Alex Williams

Alex suffered with injury but should have gone on to become England's first black goalkeeper. He worked hard, trained hard, always wanted to learn and was forever out on the training pitch with me. He had great agility, great hands and was excellent in the air. I think only I knew just how good Alex Williams actually was. He was a lovely lad, very shy and from a wonderful family. A delight to be around.

Alan Oakes

Perhaps the best left foot I've seen on a player and he scored some great goals for the club. Fit as a fiddle, honest as the day is long and a lovely guy to boot, he played more times for City than anyone else. I felt honoured when I was keeper-coach at Chester that he brought his son Michael down to train with me. I was proud that one of my peers felt I should coach his son. A fanatical golfer, I once played in a tournament with him, and, after we'd finished, he said: 'Joe, one thing about playing golf with you is that you've shown me parts of this course I didn't know existed!'

Kaziu Deyna

Maybe the best finisher I ever faced in training. He had an uncanny ability to pass the ball into the net and seemed to glide around the pitch. He was never the best trainer and would often pick up what he called 'hamstrung injury', invariably on a Monday morning, to avoid a running session. A wonderful player, a lovely man who was under enormous personal strain while he was at Maine Road. Sadly, he is no longer with us.

Joe Royle

A fantastic target man, not the quickest but as strong as a bull. I've known Joe since playing in the same England under-twenty-three side in the late Sixties. A very funny man with a dry sense of humour he always called me Desperate Dan and whenever I ordered food during an away trip, he'd tell the waiter to bring me a cow pie, complete with the horns. When he scored he'd just stand there and let people jump on him because he reckoned he'd done enough by putting the ball in the net. 'Why run around?' he would ask.

Tony Towers

What a player he should have been. I'd say he was similar to Frank Lampard in that he was up and down the pitch all game. He was a superb passer of the ball with great awareness of what was happening around him. It was a tragedy when he was allowed to go to Sunderland. He was England under-twenty-three captain and should have gone on to great things at full-international level. Had he stayed at City, who knows what heights he might have scaled.

Career Statistics

Club

Manchester City 1966–83	603 apps
Shrewsbury Town (loan) 1967	0 apps
Seattle Sounders 1983	29 apps
Brighton & Hove Albion 1984–6	36 apps
Norwich City (loan) 1985	4 apps
Stoke City (loan) 1985–6	9 apps

International honours

England (1976–82)	9 caps
England under-23 (1969)	1 app
England under-21 (1978)	3 apps
England B (1978–81)	10 apps
England XI (1981)	1 app
Football League select (1977)	1 app
FA XI (1981)	1 app

Awards

Player of the Year: Manchester City 1976, 1977, 1980

Manchester City Hall of Fame

First player to be inducted: 2004

Honours won as a player

Lancashire League Div 2 champions	1967
League Cup	1970
European Cup Winners Cup	1970
Anglo-Italian Cup runner-up	1971
League Cup	1976
Football League representative	1977
FA Cup runner-up	1981

Honours won as a coach

UEFA Cup winner (Liverpool)	2001
Super Cup winner (Liverpool)	2001
Worthington Cup winner (Liverpool)	2004

Index